Disclaimer

Specific Resources

This book intentionally does not specify particular websites, apps, or similar resources due to the vast and ever-evolving nature of such tools available online. By avoiding direct references, we aim to ensure the content remains relevant and avoids the risk of becoming outdated, encouraging readers to explore the multitude of up-to-date resources that best suit their current needs.

Financial Disclaimer

The content in "SaveMoneyOnMyBills" is for educational purposes and should not be considered as financial advice. Efforts were made to ensure accuracy, yet readers should consult with a financial advisor for personalized advice. The author and publisher will not be liable for financial decisions made based on this book's information.

Legal Disclaimer

This book does not offer legal advice. It provides general information, and laws can vary significantly by location and change over time. For legal matters, consult a qualified professional. The author and publisher disclaim liability for the use of this book's content.

General Disclaimer

"SaveMoneyOnMyBills" reflects the author's views and research, intended for informative purposes. Despite efforts for accuracy, content may not be up-to-date or applicable to all readers. The author and publisher disclaim warranties regarding the book's completeness or applicability. Users assume all risk from the book's use.

Liability Disclaimer

The author and publisher are not liable for reliance on the book's information. Readers are responsible for their decisions and are encouraged to verify the book's content independently before taking action.

Preface

Welcome to "Save Money on My Bills," a culmination of our collective knowledge, experience, and dedication to helping individuals and families navigate the often overwhelming world of personal finance. We, the team behind SaveMoneyOnMyBills.com, have spent years exploring, experimenting with, and educating others on the best practices for reducing monthly expenses and maximizing financial health.

Our journey began with a simple realization: despite the wealth of financial advice available, many people struggle to make tangible improvements to their financial situation. It's one thing to know you should be saving money; it's another to understand exactly how to do it, especially when it comes to the recurring bills that can drain your resources without you even noticing.

This book represents our commitment to bridging that gap. We've distilled the essence of our website's advice, tools, and strategies into a comprehensive guide designed to offer real, actionable solutions. Our goal is to demystify the process of reviewing and reducing your bills, providing you with a clear path to financial freedom.

Throughout these pages, you'll find a blend of practical advice, step-by-step instructions, and personal insights, all aimed at empowering you to take control of your financial destiny. We believe that by equipping you with the right knowledge and tools, we can transform the way you think about and manage your money.

"Save Money on My Bills" is more than just a book; it's a reflection of our belief in the power of informed financial decision-making. It's an invitation to join a community of individuals who refuse to accept the status quo when it comes to their finances. Whether you're a seasoned saver or just starting on your financial journey, this book is for you.

Thank you for trusting us to guide you through this process. We're excited to embark on this journey with you, confident that the strategies you're about to learn will not only reduce your monthly bills but also pave the way for a more secure and prosperous future.

Warmest regards,

The Team at SaveMoneyOnMyBills.com

Contents

How to Use This Book Effectively

To use "Save Money on My Bills" effectively, begin by assessing your current financial situation, focusing on the areas where your expenses are highest or where you feel there's the most room for improvement. Approach each chapter as a building block, implementing strategies gradually rather than trying to overhaul your finances all at once. Make use of the checklists and worksheets provided to track your progress and quantify your savings. Remember, consistency is key—regularly revisit chapters and update your approach as your financial situation evolves. Engage with the book actively, taking notes and setting actionable goals for yourself. Finally, be patient and persistent; the journey to financial freedom is a marathon, not a sprint.

Check out our website: www.SaveMoneyOnMyBills.com

Introduction

In an era where the cost of living is constantly rising, finding effective ways to manage and reduce expenses has become crucial for maintaining financial health and securing a prosperous future. "Save Money on My Bills" is not just a book; it's a comprehensive guide designed to empower readers with the knowledge, strategies, and tools needed to take control of their financial lives by meticulously reviewing and optimizing their bills.

Why is it important to review your bills and stay on top of your money? First and foremost, bills constitute a significant portion of monthly expenses for most individuals and families. Without careful review, it's easy to overlook errors, redundant services, or opportunities for savings. Additionally, staying on top of your finances by regularly reviewing your bills can prevent overpayments, help identify wasteful spending, and ensure that your money is working for you, not against you.

This book addresses the essentiality of financial vigilance, offering practical advice on negotiating better rates, eliminating unnecessary subscriptions, and making smarter choices that lead to substantial savings.

Moreover, "Save Money on My Bills" goes beyond mere cost-cutting. It aims to instill a mindset of financial mindfulness, encouraging readers to adopt habits that contribute to long-term wealth and stability. By applying the principles and techniques outlined in this book, you'll not only see immediate reductions in your monthly bills but also develop a deeper understanding of personal finance management, paving the way for lasting financial freedom.

Whether you're struggling with high utility bills, looking to cut down on subscription costs, or simply seeking ways to stretch your dollar further, this book is your roadmap to a more secure and financially savvy life. Let's embark on this journey together, transforming the way we think about and manage our bills, one page at a time.

Chapter 1: Setting the Foundation

1.1 Assessing Your Financial Health

Assessing your financial health is the critical first step toward gaining control of your finances and identifying opportunities to save money on your bills. It involves taking a comprehensive look at your income, expenses, debts, and savings to understand your current financial situation. This process allows you to set realistic goals for saving on your bills and improving your overall financial well-being. Here's a step-by-step guide, including action steps, to help you assess your financial health effectively.

Step 1: Gather Your Financial Information Begin by collecting all your financial documents and information. This includes bank statements, pay stubs, bills, credit card statements, loan documents, and any other records of income and expenses. The goal is to have a complete picture of your financial inflow and outflow.

Action Steps:

- Create a dedicated folder, either digital or physical, to organize all your financial documents.
- List all sources of income, including salaries, bonuses, and any side hustles.
- Gather all monthly bills and expenses, categorizing them as fixed (e.g., rent, mortgage, insurance) or variable (e.g., groceries, entertainment).

Step 2: Calculate Your Net Income Your net income is what you have left after taxes and deductions from your total earnings. Understanding your net income gives you a clear idea of the money you have available to cover your expenses and save.

Action Steps:

- Review your pay stubs to determine your monthly take-home pay.
- Add any other sources of income to calculate your total monthly net income.

Step 3: Track and Categorize Your Spending Identify where your money goes each month by categorizing your spending. Common categories include housing, utilities, food, transportation, insurance, debts, savings, and entertainment.

Action Steps:

- Use your gathered financial documents to list all your expenses under the relevant categories.
- Utilize budgeting apps or spreadsheets to track and categorize your spending for better visualization.

Step 4: Analyze Your Debt Situation Debt plays a significant role in your financial health. Identify all your debts, including credit card debt, student loans, auto loans, and any other debts. Note down the interest rates, monthly payment amounts, and due dates for each debt.

Action Steps:

- Create a debt list, including lender names, balance owed, interest rates, and monthly payments.
- Prioritize your debts, considering factors like interest rates and balances.

Step 5: Evaluate Your Savings and Emergency Fund Assessing your savings and the status of your emergency fund is crucial. An emergency fund is essential for financial security, ideally covering 3-6 months of living expenses.

Action Steps:

- Calculate your total savings, including all savings accounts, investment accounts, and other liquid assets.
- Review your emergency fund to ensure it's adequate for unexpected expenses or financial downturns.

Step 6: Set Financial Goals Based on your assessment, set specific, measurable, achievable, relevant, and time-bound (SMART) financial goals. These could include increasing your savings rate, paying down debt, or cutting unnecessary expenses.

Action Steps:

- Write down your financial goals, making them as specific as possible.
- Create a timeline for achieving each goal, with milestones to track your progress.

Conclusion: Assessing your financial health is an ongoing process. Regularly review and adjust your budget, spending habits, and financial goals to ensure you're on track. Remember, the key to improving your financial health and saving money on your bills lies in understanding your finances and making informed decisions based on that knowledge.

1.2 Understanding Your Bills

Gaining a thorough understanding of your bills is essential for managing your finances effectively and identifying opportunities to cut costs. This process involves more than just knowing how much you owe each month; it requires a deep dive into each bill to understand the services you're paying for, the terms of those services, and any potential areas where you can reduce costs.

Follow this step-by-step guide, complete with action steps and a checklist, to master your bills and optimize your spending.

Step 1: Compile All Your Bills Start by gathering every bill you receive on a regular, semi-regular, and irregular basis. This includes utilities, rent or mortgage, insurance premiums, subscription services, credit card statements, and any other recurring charges.

Action Steps:

- Collect the latest statement for each bill.
- For bills not received monthly, note the period they cover and their due dates.

Checklist:

- ✓ Utility bills (electricity, gas, water, sewage)
- ✓ Housing payments (rent, mortgage)
- ✓ Insurance policies (health, auto, home, life)
- ✓ Subscription services (streaming media, magazines, software)
- ✓ Credit card bills
- ✓ Loan payments (student, personal, auto)
- ✓ Internet and phone services

Step 2: Analyze Each Bill Individually For each bill, examine the details of what you're being charged. Look for usage charges, base fees, taxes, and any additional fees or services that you may not be fully utilizing.

Action Steps:

- Highlight or list all the components of each bill.
- Identify any charges you do not understand or recognize.

Step 3: Research Alternative Options For services such as internet, phone, insurance, and subscriptions, investigate alternative providers or plans that may offer a better value for the same service or less.

Action Steps:

- Compare plans from different providers.
- Check for promotions, discounts, or bundles that could reduce your costs.

Step 4: Identify Potential Savings Based on your analysis, pinpoint where you could potentially save money. This could involve switching plans or providers, canceling unnecessary services, or negotiating better rates.

Action Steps:

- Mark services you can live without or downgrade.
- Prepare to negotiate bills by researching competitive rates and being ready to switch providers if necessary.

Step 5: Take Action to Reduce Costs Implement the changes you've identified to lower your expenses. This may involve contacting service providers to negotiate, switching plans or providers, or canceling services.

Action Steps:

- Contact service providers with a plan to negotiate or inquire about less expensive options.
- If negotiation fails, be prepared to switch providers.
- Officially cancel any services you no longer need.

Step 6: Monitor and Adjust After making changes, monitor your bills in the following months to ensure that the expected savings materialize. Keep an eye out for any new charges and adjust your plans as necessary.

Action Steps:

- Review your bills monthly to confirm savings.
- Stay informed about new deals or changes in rates.

Conclusion: Understanding your bills in detail empowers you to make informed decisions about your spending. By taking a proactive approach to analyze, research, and adjust your expenses, you can optimize your finances and potentially save a significant amount of money. Regularly revisiting your bills ensures that you remain in control of your financial health and continue to identify savings opportunities.

1.3 The Psychology of Spending and Saving

Understanding the psychology behind your spending and saving habits is pivotal to gaining control over your finances. Our financial decisions are often influenced by emotions, habits, and cognitive biases, making it important to reflect on these aspects to foster healthier financial behaviors.

This section will guide you through a self-assessment to uncover your spending triggers, savings attitudes, and how you can leverage this understanding to improve your financial well-being.

Step 1: Reflect on Your Spending Habits Begin by observing your spending patterns without judgment. Look for patterns in when and why you spend money, particularly in moments of stress, happiness, or boredom.

Action Steps:

- Keep a spending diary for a month, noting what you bought, how much it cost, and what you were feeling or thinking at the time of purchase.
- Review your diary to identify any emotional triggers linked to spending.

Self-Assessment Questions:

- Do I spend more when I'm feeling a certain way (e.g., stressed, happy, sad)?
- Are there specific times of day, week, or situations where I'm more likely to spend?

Step 2: Analyze Your Savings Attitudes Reflect on your feelings and beliefs about saving money. Understanding your mindset towards savings can reveal what might be holding you back from saving more effectively.

Action Steps:

- Write down your thoughts about saving money. Do you find it rewarding, necessary, challenging, or something else?
- Consider any experiences that might have shaped these attitudes.

Self-Assessment Questions:

- How do I feel when I think about saving money?
- What beliefs do I hold about money that could be influencing my saving habits?

Step 3: Identify Cognitive Biases We're all susceptible to cognitive biases that can affect our financial decisions. Common biases include the "instant gratification" bias, where immediate rewards are valued more highly than future gains, or the "status quo" bias, where we prefer to keep things as they are.

Action Steps:

- Reflect on recent financial decisions and identify if any biases were at play.
- Acknowledge these biases and consider how they influence your spending and saving.

Self-Assessment Questions:

- Do I tend to choose immediate pleasures over long-term benefits?
- Am I sticking to financial habits just because they're familiar, even if they're not beneficial?

Step 4: Set Goals Based on Your Assessment Using the insights from your self-assessment, set specific, achievable financial goals that address your psychological tendencies. This could involve creating a budget, setting up automatic savings, or finding healthier ways to cope with emotional triggers.

Action Steps:

- Based on your spending triggers and attitudes towards saving, define clear financial goals.
- Create a plan that incorporates strategies to overcome psychological barriers, such as setting up automatic savings for future gains or establishing a reward system for meeting savings goals.

Step 5: Implement and Monitor Put your plan into action and monitor your progress. Adjust your strategies as needed, keeping in mind the psychological insights you've gained.

Action Steps:

- Implement one financial change at a time to monitor its impact on your spending and saving habits.
- Regularly review your financial diary and goals to assess progress and make adjustments.

Conclusion: Understanding the psychology behind your financial decisions is a powerful step towards improving your spending and saving habits. By conducting this self-assessment and implementing targeted strategies, you can work towards a healthier financial future. Remember, change takes time, and self-awareness is the first step toward lasting financial well-being.

Chapter 2: Basic Strategies for Saving on Bills

2.1 Budgeting for Success: A Step-by-Step Guide

Mastering the art of budgeting is essential for achieving financial stability and realizing your savings goals. A well-crafted budget helps you understand where your money is going, ensures you can cover your essential bills, and facilitates saving for the future. This guide will walk you through creating a budget, complemented by action steps and a downloadable budgeting worksheet to help you put your plan into action.

Step 1: Calculate Your Monthly Income Start by determining your total monthly income after taxes. Include all sources of income such as salaries, bonuses, freelance work, and any passive income streams.

Action Steps:

- List all income sources on the budgeting worksheet.
- Use your net income for accuracy, ensuring all calculations are after-tax.

Step 2: List Your Monthly Expenses Track and categorize your expenses into fixed and variable. Fixed expenses are those that remain relatively constant each month, such as rent or mortgage, insurance premiums, and loan payments. Variable expenses include groceries, entertainment, and personal spending.

Action Steps:

- Refer to bank statements and receipts to ensure all expenses are accounted for.
- Categorize each expense as either fixed or variable on your worksheet.

Step 3: Prioritize Your Spending After listing your expenses, prioritize them based on necessity. Essentials like housing, food, and healthcare should be at the top, followed by savings, and then non-essential but desirable expenses.

Action Steps:

- Mark essential expenses clearly on your worksheet.
- Allocate funds to savings immediately after essential expenses to emphasize its importance.

Step 4: Set Savings and Debt Repayment Goals Decide how much you want to save each month or what percentage of your income you want to put towards savings and debt repayment. These goals should be realistic and achievable, considering your essential expenses and income.

Action Steps:

- Determine a fixed amount or percentage of your income for savings and debt repayment.
- Include these as fixed commitments in your budgeting worksheet.

Step 5: Adjust Expenses to Meet Your Financial Goals If your expenses exceed your income, or if there's little left for savings, look for areas to cut back. This might mean reducing discretionary spending, finding cheaper alternatives for services, or canceling unused subscriptions.

Action Steps:

- Highlight areas in your variable expenses where cuts can be made.
- Research cheaper alternatives for high-cost fixed expenses, such as insurance or phone plans.

Step 6: Implement Your Budget With your budget planned, the next step is to put it into practice. Monitor your spending throughout the month to ensure it aligns with your budget. Adjustments may be necessary as you fine-tune your spending habits.

Action Steps:

- Use apps or spreadsheets to track your spending in real-time.
- Review your budget weekly to catch and correct any deviations early.

Step 7: Review and Adjust Monthly Your budget is a living document that should evolve as your financial situation and goals change. Regularly review your budget to reflect changes in income, expenses, or financial priorities.

Action Steps:

- At the end of each month, review your spending, savings, and whether you met your financial goals.
- Adjust your budget for the next month based on your review.

Conclusion: Budgeting is a powerful tool for managing your finances and working towards your financial goals. By following these steps and utilizing the budgeting worksheet, you can create a budget that not only reflects your current financial situation but also guides you towards future success. Remember, the key to successful budgeting is consistency and willingness to adjust as your financial situation evolves.

2.2 **Negotiating Lower Rates: Complete with Scripts**

Negotiating lower rates on your bills can lead to significant savings over time. Whether it's your credit card interest rate, insurance premiums, or cable bill, many companies are willing to negotiate rates to retain loyal customers. This guide will walk you through the process of negotiating lower rates, including actionable steps, scripts for conversations, and a worksheet to prepare for negotiations.

Preparation

Step 1: Gather Information Before you start negotiating, collect all relevant information about your account, including your account number, current rate or premium, and details of any competitive offers you've found.

Action Steps:

- Compile your latest statements and any promotional materials or offers from competitors.
- Research competitors' rates for similar services or products.

Step 2: Determine Your Negotiation Points Identify why you deserve a lower rate. This could be your loyalty to the company, a clean payment history, or better offers from competitors.

Action Steps:

- List your reasons for deserving a lower rate.
- Prepare to mention any competitive offers as leverage.

Step 3: Understand Your Goals Know the rate you're aiming for but be realistic based on the research you've conducted.

Action Steps:

- Set a target rate that is competitive yet reasonable.
- Decide on your minimum acceptable rate before walking away or considering cancellation.

The Negotiation Process

Step 4: Make the Call Initiate contact with your service provider, armed with your research and points of negotiation.

Script Example: "Hi, my name is [Your Name], and I've been a customer with [Company Name] for [number of years]. I recently reviewed my current rates and found that I might be paying more than necessary. I've seen some competitive offers from other companies. Could we discuss my current rate and see if there's a possibility to adjust it?"

Step 5: Use Leverage Wisely If the representative seems resistant to offering a lower rate, mention the competitive offers you've found, emphasizing your preference to stay with your current provider if a better rate can be negotiated.

Script Example: "I really enjoy the service and would prefer to stay. However, [Competitor] is offering a similar service at a significantly lower rate. Is there anything you can do to match this or offer a better rate?"

Step 6: Be Prepared to Escalate If the first representative cannot help, ask politely to speak with a manager or someone in the loyalty or retention department, as they often have more authority to offer discounts.

Script Example: "I understand your limitations, but I believe this matter is important. Could I please speak with a manager or someone from the retention department who might have more flexibility with rates?"

After the Negotiation

Step 7: Confirm and Document Once you've reached an agreement, confirm the new rate and ask for it in writing. Ensure you understand any new terms associated with the rate.

Action Steps:

- Confirm the details of the new agreement verbally.
- Request an email or letter confirming the new rate and any terms.

Step 8: Update Your Worksheet Keep a negotiation worksheet where you log each negotiation attempt, outcomes, and any follow-up actions needed.

Worksheet Columns:

- Date of negotiation
- Service provider
- Original rate
- Offered rate
- Competitive offers mentioned
- Final agreed rate
- Follow-up actions

Conclusion

Negotiating lower rates requires preparation, persistence, and patience. By following these steps and using the provided scripts, you'll be better equipped to negotiate effectively. Remember, the worst outcome is a simple "no," but the potential savings are worth the effort.

2.3 **Cutting Unnecessary Expenses**

Reducing unnecessary expenses is an effective way to improve your financial health and free up funds for savings or paying down debt. This guide provides a structured approach to identify and eliminate non-essential spending, along with action steps and a tracking worksheet to help you monitor your progress.

Step 1: Identify Your Expenses

Action Steps:

- List all your monthly expenses. Use bank statements, receipts, and credit card statements from the past month to ensure you capture everything.
- Categorize your expenses into 'needs' (essentials like rent, groceries, utilities) and 'wants' (non-essentials like dining out, subscriptions, luxury items).

Step 2: Evaluate Your Spending

Action Steps:

- Review each 'want' expense to determine its importance and joy it brings to your life.
- Ask yourself, "Can I live without this?" and "How often do I actually use this service or product?"

Step 3: Set Reduction Goals

Action Steps:

- For each non-essential expense identified, set a goal for reduction or elimination. For instance, reduce dining out from four times a month to once.
- Prioritize reductions based on potential savings and impact on your lifestyle.

Step 4: Implement Changes

Action Steps:

- Cancel any subscriptions or memberships you no longer use or need. Many services make cancellation challenging, so be persistent.
- Switch to cheaper alternatives for some services. For example, use a streaming service instead of cable TV.
- Adopt cost-saving habits, such as cooking at home more often instead of dining out.

Step 5: Use a Tracking Worksheet

Action Steps:

- Create a tracking worksheet to monitor your expenses and the changes you implement. This can be a simple spreadsheet with columns for the expense name, category ('need' or 'want'), current cost, reduced cost, and savings.
- Update the worksheet monthly to track your progress and adjust your goals as needed.

Step 6: Evaluate and Adjust

Action Steps:

- At the end of each month, review your tracking worksheet. Examine where you succeeded in cutting expenses and where you fell short.
- Use this insight to adjust your goals and strategies for the next month. If you find that certain cuts are too challenging to maintain, consider other areas where you might be able to reduce spending.

Step 7: Reinforce Your Successes

Action Steps:

- Celebrate your successes in reducing unnecessary expenses. Recognizing your achievements, no matter how small, can provide motivation to continue.
- Consider reallocating some of your savings toward a reward for yourself, such as a small purchase or experience that brings you joy, or toward increasing your savings or investment contributions.

Conclusion

Cutting unnecessary expenses is a dynamic process that requires regular review and adjustment. By methodically identifying non-essential spending, setting clear reduction goals, and tracking your progress, you can significantly improve your financial situation. Remember, the goal isn't to deprive yourself but to make conscious decisions about your spending to achieve a more secure and enjoyable financial future.

2.4 The Art of Comparison Shopping

Comparison shopping is a critical skill that can save you a significant amount of money on regular purchases and bills. By evaluating your options and comparing prices and features across different products or service providers, you can make more informed decisions that align with your financial goals. This guide will outline actionable steps to master comparison shopping and includes a template for a comparison chart to help you organize your findings.

Step 1: Identify Your Needs and Preferences

Before you start comparing, clearly define what you need from the product or service. Consider factors such as quality, features, warranty, customer service, and specific preferences that are important to you.

Action Steps:

- List the essential features or services you need.
- Note any preferences or deal-breakers.

Step 2: Research Your Options

Gather information on all the available options that meet your criteria. Use a variety of sources including online reviews, consumer reports, and recommendations from friends or family to get a comprehensive view.

Action Steps:

- Search for products or services that match your needs.
- Create a list of potential options.

Step 3: Use a Comparison Chart

Create a comparison chart to organize the information you've gathered. This chart should allow you to compare features, prices, pros and cons, and any other relevant details side-by-side.

Comparison Chart Template:

Feature/Provider	Option 1	Option 2	Option 3	Option 4
Price				
Features				
Customer Reviews				
Warranty				
Availability				
Additional Costs				

Action Steps:

- Fill in the chart with information for each option.
- Highlight any significant differences or standout features.

Step 4: Evaluate Total Costs

Consider not only the upfront cost but also any additional expenses associated with each option, such as shipping, installation, or maintenance fees.

Action Steps:

- Calculate the total cost of ownership for each option.
- Note these costs in your comparison chart for a direct comparison.

Step 5: Assess Value and Quality

Price isn't the only factor to consider; assess the value and quality of each option. Sometimes, paying a bit more upfront can save money in the long run due to better durability or lower operating costs.

Action Steps:

- Read reviews and consumer feedback to gauge the quality and reliability.
- Consider the longevity and any savings from lower maintenance or operating costs.

Step 6: Make Your Decision

Use the information in your comparison chart to make an informed decision. Choose the option that offers the best combination of price, quality, and features that meet your needs.

Action Steps:

- Review your comparison chart and weigh the pros and cons.
- Decide which option best fits your criteria and budget.

Step 7: Monitor Your Purchase

After making your purchase, keep an eye on the product or service performance to ensure it meets your expectations. This can also provide valuable information for future comparison shopping.

Action Steps:

- Note any discrepancies between expected and actual performance or service.
- Consider this experience in future comparison shopping endeavors.

Conclusion

Mastering the art of comparison shopping can significantly impact your financial well-being by ensuring you always get the best value for your money. By following these steps and utilizing the comparison chart template, you can systematically evaluate your options and make choices that align with your financial goals and personal preferences.

Chapter 3: Saving on Utility Bills

3.1 Reducing Electricity Consumption

Cutting down on electricity consumption is not only good for the environment but also for your wallet. With the right strategies and a little diligence, you can significantly reduce your energy bills. This guide will provide actionable steps to reduce electricity consumption and include an Energy Use Worksheet to help track and manage your energy savings.

Step 1: Conduct an Energy Audit

Start by understanding where and how electricity is used in your home. You can do this by conducting a simple energy audit which will identify areas for improvement.

Action Steps:

- Use a home energy audit checklist available online or from your local utility provider.
- Inspect your home for any leaks, outdated appliances, or inefficient lighting, noting these on your audit list.

Step 2: Implement Quick Wins

Address simple changes that can yield immediate savings with minimal effort or investment.

Action Steps:

- Replace incandescent bulbs with LED lights.
- Unplug chargers and appliances when not in use.
- Use power strips to easily switch off electronics.

Step 3: Optimize Heating and Cooling

Heating and cooling can account for a large portion of your energy bill. Optimizing these systems can lead to significant savings.

Action Steps:

- Set your thermostat to energy-saving settings (e.g., 78°F in summer, 68°F in winter).
- Seal windows and doors to prevent leaks.
- Clean or replace HVAC filters regularly.

Step 4: Use Appliances and Electronics Efficiently

Appliances and electronics can consume a lot of energy, but efficient use can help reduce their impact.

Action Steps:

- Only run dishwashers and washing machines with full loads.
- Use energy-saving settings on appliances.
- Consider air drying clothes instead of using the dryer.

Step 5: Invest in Energy-Efficient Appliances

When it's time to replace or buy new appliances, choosing energy-efficient models can result in long-term savings.

Action Steps:

- Look for the ENERGY STAR label when purchasing new appliances.
- Compare energy use using the Energy Guide labels.

Step 6: Track and Adjust Your Energy Use

Use an Energy Use Worksheet to track your consumption and identify areas for further savings.

Energy Use Worksheet Template:

Appliance/Usage	Current Consumption	Target Reduction	Action Taken	New Consumption	Savings
Lighting					
Heating					
Cooling					
Electronics					
Appliances					

Action Steps:

- Fill in your current monthly consumption for each category.
- Set realistic targets for reduction.
- Note the actions you've taken to reduce consumption.
- After implementing changes, fill in the new consumption to calculate savings.

Conclusion

Reducing electricity consumption requires a combination of immediate actions and long-term changes in habits and investments in efficient appliances. By systematically following these steps and using the Energy Use Worksheet to track your progress, you can manage your energy consumption more effectively, leading to significant savings on your electricity bills. Remember, the key to success is not just in making changes but in maintaining energy-efficient habits over time.

3.2 Water Conservation Methods

Water conservation is an essential practice for both environmental sustainability and reducing household expenses. Implementing effective water-saving techniques can significantly decrease your water bill and contribute to the preservation of this vital resource. This guide offers actionable steps to conserve water in your household, accompanied by a conservation checklist for tracking your progress.

Understanding Your Water Usage

Step 1: Analyze Your Water Bill Begin by reviewing your current water usage as listed on your utility bill. Understanding your baseline consumption is crucial for setting targets and measuring progress.

Action Steps:

- Locate the section of your water bill that details consumption in gallons or cubic meters.
- Note any seasonal fluctuations or trends in your water use.

Implementing Basic Water-Saving Practices

Step 2: Fix Leaks Promptly A single dripping faucet or leaking toilet can waste a significant amount of water over time.

Action Steps:

- Regularly check faucets, pipes, and toilets for leaks.
- Replace worn washers and gaskets as soon as leaks are detected.

Step 3: Upgrade to Low-Flow Fixtures Installing water-efficient fixtures can drastically reduce water use without sacrificing performance.

Action Steps:

- Replace old showerheads with low-flow models.
- Install low-flow aerators on faucets.

Optimizing Water Use in Daily Activities

Step 4: Adopt Efficient Water Practices in the Bathroom The bathroom is one of the highest water-use areas in the home.

Action Steps:

- Take shorter showers and consider showering less frequently.
- Turn off the tap while brushing your teeth or shaving.

Step 5: Be Water-Wise in the Kitchen Kitchen activities, including dishwashing and food preparation, offer significant opportunities for water savings.

Action Steps:

- Only run the dishwasher with a full load and choose the eco-setting if available.
- Wash fruits and vegetables in a bowl of water instead of under running water.

Step 6: Practice Sustainable Landscaping Outdoor watering can account for a large portion of residential water use, especially in warmer months.

Action Steps:

- ✓ Water your garden during the early morning or late evening to reduce evaporation.
- ✓ Use drought-resistant plants and mulch to retain soil moisture.

Water Conservation Checklist

To help you implement and track these water-saving measures, use the following checklist:

- ✓ Checked for and repaired any leaks in faucets, toilets, and pipes.
- ✓ Installed low-flow showerheads and faucet aerators.
- ✓ Adopted water-efficient practices in the bathroom.
- • Optimized kitchen water use by adjusting dishwashing and food preparation habits.
- • Implemented sustainable landscaping practices to minimize outdoor water use.

Monitoring and Adjusting Your Water Use

Step 7: Review Your Water Bill Regularly Continuously monitor your water bill to assess the impact of your conservation efforts and identify areas for further improvement.

Action Steps:

- • Compare current consumption to previous periods.
- • Set new targets for water use reduction based on your progress.

Conclusion

Water conservation is a continuous process that requires commitment and incremental changes to daily habits. By following these steps and utilizing the water conservation checklist, you can significantly reduce your water usage, lower your bills, and contribute to environmental sustainability. Remember, every drop saved contributes to the larger goal of preserving our planet's precious water resources.

3.3 Smart Heating and Cooling

Optimizing your home's heating and cooling systems is one of the most effective ways to reduce energy consumption and lower your utility bills. Smart heating and cooling strategies not only enhance your home's comfort but also contribute to environmental conservation. This guide provides actionable steps for smart heating and cooling, accompanied by a savings calculator to help estimate your cost savings.

Step 1: Conduct an Energy Efficiency Assessment

Action Steps:

- Inspect your heating and cooling systems for any signs of inefficiency, such as outdated equipment or poor maintenance.
- Consider hiring a professional to perform an energy audit, identifying areas for improvement in insulation, ductwork, and system efficiency.

Step 2: Install Programmable or Smart Thermostats

Programmable thermostats allow you to set your heating and cooling systems to operate only when needed, avoiding unnecessary energy consumption.

Action Steps:

- Purchase a programmable or smart thermostat that suits your heating and cooling systems.
- Set the thermostat to lower (in winter) or raise (in summer) the temperature during times when you are asleep or away from home.

Step 3: Improve Home Insulation

Proper insulation reduces the workload on your heating and cooling systems by maintaining your home's temperature.

Action Steps:

- Check and upgrade insulation in key areas such as the attic, walls, floors, and basements.
- Seal gaps and leaks around doors, windows, and any other areas where air may escape.

Step 4: Utilize Energy-Efficient Windows and Window Treatments

Windows play a crucial role in regulating your home's temperature by preventing heat loss in winter and blocking heat gain in summer.

Action Steps:

- Install double-glazed or energy-efficient windows.
- Use curtains, blinds, and shades to control sunlight and heat entering your home.

Step 5: Maintain Your Heating and Cooling Systems

Regular maintenance of your heating and cooling systems ensures they operate efficiently and last longer.

Action Steps:

- Replace or clean filters regularly.
- Schedule annual maintenance checks with a qualified technician.

Step 6: Adopt Natural Ventilation and Cooling Techniques

Before resorting to air conditioning, try natural methods to cool your home, which can significantly reduce your energy usage.

Action Steps:

- Open windows in the early morning and late evening to allow cool air to circulate.
- Use ceiling fans to enhance air movement and comfort levels.

Step 7: Use the Savings Calculator

To estimate the savings from implementing smart heating and cooling strategies, use a simple savings calculator. Your utility company should have a calculator readily available for your use on their website. This tool can help you understand the financial benefits of your energy efficiency improvements.

Savings Calculator Inputs:

- Current monthly heating and cooling costs.
- Estimated percentage reduction in energy consumption from each action step.
- Cost of upgrades or improvements (for calculating payback period).

Action Steps:

- Input your current heating and cooling costs and estimated savings percentages into the calculator.
- Calculate your expected monthly savings and payback period for any investments in energy efficiency.

Conclusion

Adopting smart heating and cooling practices is an effective way to enhance your home's comfort, reduce energy consumption, and save on utility bills. By following these actionable steps and using a savings calculator, you can make informed decisions about which strategies will offer the best return on investment for your specific situation. Remember, small changes can lead to significant savings over time, benefiting both your wallet and the environment.

3.4 Leveraging Renewable Energy

Incorporating renewable energy into your home or personal life not only contributes to environmental conservation but can also offer significant long-term financial savings. This guide outlines the steps to research and evaluate renewable energy options, like solar panels or wind turbines, and includes a cost-benefit worksheet to help assess the financial viability of such investments.

Step 1: Identify Your Renewable Energy Options

Start by exploring the types of renewable energy sources suitable for your geographical area and property type. Common options include solar panels, wind turbines, and geothermal systems.

Action Steps:

- Research online resources or consult with local environmental agencies to identify viable renewable energy sources in your area.
- Consider your property's exposure to sunlight, wind patterns, and geothermal potential as relevant.

Step 2: Research Incentives and Rebates

Many governments and utilities offer incentives, rebates, or tax credits to encourage the adoption of renewable energy. These can significantly reduce the upfront costs.

Action Steps:

- Visit government and utility websites or consult with a renewable energy professional to learn about available incentives in your area.
- Take note of application deadlines and eligibility criteria for these incentives.

Step 3: Evaluate Your Energy Needs

Understanding your current and future energy needs is crucial for selecting an appropriately sized renewable energy system.

Action Steps:

- Review your past utility bills to determine your average energy consumption.
- Consider future changes, such as family growth or the addition of an electric vehicle, which might affect your energy requirements.

Step 4: Obtain Quotes from Renewable Energy Providers

To get a clear picture of the potential costs, obtain quotes from multiple reputable renewable energy system providers.

Action Steps:

- Request detailed quotes that include the cost of equipment, installation, and any ongoing maintenance.
- Ensure the quotes also outline the expected energy output of the systems to calculate potential savings accurately.

Step 5: Use the Cost-Benefit Worksheet

A cost-benefit worksheet helps you to quantitatively assess the financial implications of investing in renewable energy.

Cost-Benefit Worksheet Components:

- **System Cost**: The total upfront cost of purchasing and installing the renewable energy system.
- **Incentives/Rebates**: The value of any incentives or rebates you can apply, reducing the effective system cost.

- **Annual Energy Savings**: Estimated savings on your energy bills as a result of using the renewable energy system.
- **Payback Period**: The time it takes for the energy savings to cover the net system cost.
- **Long-Term Savings**: Projected savings over the lifespan of the system beyond the payback period.

Action Steps:

- Fill in the worksheet with the information gathered from your research and quotes.
- Calculate the payback period and long-term savings to assess the financial benefit of the investment.

Step 6: Make an Informed Decision

Based on your research and the cost-benefit analysis, decide whether investing in renewable energy is right for you at this time.

Action Steps:

- Consider not only the financial aspects but also the environmental benefits and your personal values regarding sustainable living.
- If you decide to proceed, select the renewable energy option that offers the best balance of cost-effectiveness, energy efficiency, and reliability.

Step 7: Plan for Implementation

Once you've made the decision to invest in renewable energy, plan for the implementation process.

Action Steps:

- Finalize agreements with your chosen provider, ensuring all incentives and rebates are correctly applied.
- Prepare for the installation process, which may include obtaining permits and scheduling the work.

Conclusion

Adopting renewable energy can be a rewarding decision, offering both financial savings and environmental benefits. By systematically researching your options, assessing your energy needs, understanding available incentives, and conducting a thorough cost-benefit analysis, you can make an informed decision that aligns with your financial goals and sustainable living values. This structured approach ensures that you consider all aspects of the investment, leading to a more sustainable and financially sound future.

Chapter 4: Telecommunications Savings

4.1 Choosing the Right Cell Phone Plan

Selecting the right cell phone plan can be a daunting task given the myriad of options available. However, by methodically comparing plans based on your specific needs and usage patterns, you can make an informed decision that saves you money and meets your communication requirements. This guide provides a step-by-step approach to choosing the best cell phone plan, including a comparison chart and a decision worksheet to simplify the process.

Step 1: Assess Your Usage Needs

Before you start comparing plans, it's crucial to understand your cell phone usage patterns and preferences.

Action Steps:

- Track your data usage over the past few months to determine how many gigabytes you typically use.
- Consider your needs for call minutes and text messages.
- Think about any additional features you require, such as international calling or hotspot data.

Step 2: Research Available Plans

Once you have a clear understanding of your needs, begin researching cell phone plans offered by different carriers. Pay attention to the coverage in your area to ensure reliable service.

Action Steps:

- List down the major carriers and any regional providers offering service in your area.
- Gather information on their plans, including data limits, call and text allowances, prices, and any additional benefits.

Step 3: Use a Comparison Chart

To effectively compare cell phone plans, create a comparison chart that lays out the key features and costs side by side.

Comparison Chart Template:

Feature/Carrier	Plan 1	Plan 2	Plan 3	Notes
Monthly Cost				
Data Allowance				
Call Minutes				
Text Messages				
International				
Additional Fees				
Special Offers				

Action Steps:

- Fill in the chart with details from the plans you're considering.
- Highlight any plans that seem to fit your usage needs and budget.

Step 4: Evaluate Additional Factors

Beyond the basic costs and allowances, consider other factors that might influence your decision, such as customer service, network reliability, and the flexibility of the plan.

Action Steps:

- Read customer reviews and independent ratings for insight into each carrier's service quality.
- Check the carrier's policy on changing plans or fees for exceeding limits.

Step 5: Use the Decision Worksheet

To finalize your decision, use a worksheet that helps you weigh the pros and cons of each plan based on your comparison chart.

Decision Worksheet Components:

- **Personal Usage Fit:** How well does each plan meet your data, call, and text needs?
- **Cost-Effectiveness:** Is the plan priced competitively for the services offered?
- **Carrier Reputation:** Based on reviews and ratings, how reliable is the carrier?
- **Flexibility and Terms:** Are there any deal-breakers in the plan's terms and conditions?

Action Steps:

- Score each plan in the worksheet categories based on your priorities.
- Tally the scores to identify which plan offers the best combination of value, service, and fit for your needs.

Step 6: Make Your Decision

Review the scores and insights from your comparison chart and decision worksheet. Choose the plan that offers the best overall value according to your specific needs and preferences.

Conclusion

Choosing the right cell phone plan requires a clear understanding of your usage patterns, thorough research, and careful comparison of your options. By following these steps and utilizing the provided tools, you can confidently select a cell phone plan that offers the best balance of cost, coverage, and features tailored to your

4.2 Reducing Internet and Cable Bills

In today's digital age, internet and cable services are nearly indispensable, but they can also form a significant portion of monthly expenses. Fortunately, with the right approach, you can negotiate lower rates and optimize these services to better fit your budget. This guide outlines actionable steps to reduce your internet and cable bills, complete with negotiation scripts and a savings tracker to help monitor your progress.

Step 1: Assess Your Current Services

Begin by thoroughly reviewing your current internet and cable plans. Understand what you're paying for, including any bundled services, to identify potential areas for savings.

Action Steps:

- List all the features of your current plans, including speed, data limits, channel packages, and any additional services.
- Evaluate which services you actually use and which could be eliminated or downgraded.

Step 2: Research Competing Offers

Before entering negotiations, arm yourself with information about what other providers are offering. This knowledge can serve as powerful leverage during discussions.

Action Steps:

- Research competitors' pricing for similar services in your area.
- Look for promotions, discounts, or lower-priced plans that meet your needs.

Step 3: Prepare Your Negotiation Strategy

With a clear understanding of your current usage and alternative options, develop your negotiation strategy. Decide on the outcomes you're aiming for, such as a reduced rate or more favorable terms.

Action Steps:

- Prioritize your negotiation goals (e.g., lowering your bill, increasing service features).
- Prepare to reference specific competitor offers that support your case for a lower rate.

Step 4: Contact Customer Service

Reach out to your provider's customer service or retention department, prepared to discuss your account and express your concerns about the current rate.

Negotiation Script: *"Hello, my name is [Your Name], and I've been reviewing my current internet and cable services. I noticed that I'm paying quite a bit, especially when I see that [Competitor] offers similar services at a lower price. I've been a loyal customer, and I'd like to discuss options for reducing my bill while maintaining the great service I've come to expect."*

Step 5: Leverage Competitor Offers

If the representative is hesitant to offer a discount, mention the specific deals you've found from competitors. This demonstrates that you have options and are considering a switch.

Negotiation Script: "*I appreciate the value your service provides, but I'm finding it difficult to justify the expense when [Competitor] is offering [specific deal] for new customers. Is there a way we can adjust my current plan to better reflect these market rates?*"

Step 6: Review and Confirm Any Offer

Once you've reached an agreement, ensure you understand the terms. Ask for a confirmation via email or letter, detailing the new rate and any changes to your service.

Action Steps:

- Confirm the specifics of the new offer, including the duration of any promotional rates.
- Ask for the agreement in writing for your records.

Step 7: Track Your Savings

Use a savings tracker to monitor the impact of your negotiations on your monthly bills. This can also help plan future financial strategies.

Savings Tracker Components:	
Date of Negotiation	
Original Monthly Bill	
Monthly Savings	
Negotiated Monthly Bill	
Notes on the Agreement	

Action Steps:

- Update the tracker each month to reflect your actual savings.
- Reevaluate your services and the market before any promotional rates expire to prepare for future negotiations.

Conclusion

Reducing your internet and cable bills through negotiation requires preparation, clarity on your desired outcomes, and persistence. By following these steps and utilizing the provided scripts and savings tracker, you can effectively lower your monthly expenses and ensure you're getting the best value for your services. Remember, providers are often willing to offer discounts or adjust plans to retain customers, so don't hesitate to advocate for a more affordable rate.

4.2 Evaluating your Viewing Habits

In recent years, the shift from traditional cable TV to streaming services has gained significant momentum. "Cutting the cord" refers to canceling cable or satellite subscriptions in favor of internet-based streaming options.

This approach can offer more flexibility and often, substantial savings. This guide provides a step-by-step plan for evaluating alternatives to cable, including an options guide and a cost analysis worksheet to help you make an informed decision.

Step 1: Evaluate Your Viewing Habits

Before making any changes, assess your current viewing habits and what you value most in a television service.

Action Steps:

- List your must-have channels, shows, and the type of content you enjoy.
- Note how often you watch live TV versus on-demand content.

Step 2: Research Streaming Services

Explore the wide range of streaming services available, noting which ones offer the content you enjoy.

Action Steps:

- Compile a list of streaming services, such as Netflix, Hulu, Amazon Prime Video, Disney+, and specialized platforms like HBO Max or ESPN+.
- For each service, list the available content, monthly cost, and any additional features like offline viewing or multiple simultaneous streams.

Step 3: Consider Live TV Streaming Options

If live TV is important to you, look into live TV streaming services as a direct replacement for cable.

Action Steps:

- Identify live TV streaming services such as YouTube TV, Sling TV, and Hulu + Live TV.
- Check their channel lineups, pricing, and any restrictions like DVR capabilities or simultaneous streams.

Step 4: Assess Internet Requirements

Streaming quality video requires a reliable and fast internet connection. Ensure your current internet service meets these needs.

Action Steps:

- Determine the internet speed required for high-quality streaming (at least 25 Mbps for 4K streaming).
- If necessary, research options to upgrade your internet service, considering the added cost against potential cable savings.

Step 5: Use a Cost Analysis Worksheet

To compare the costs of streaming services versus traditional cable, utilize a cost analysis worksheet. This tool will help you visualize potential savings.

Cost Analysis Worksheet Components:

- **Current Cable Bill**: Include monthly rate, rental fees, and any additional costs.
- **Streaming Service Options**: List each service you're considering, along with the monthly cost.
- **Internet Service Upgrade (if needed)**: Include the cost of upgrading your internet service.
- **Total Monthly Cost**: Calculate the total cost of streaming services and any additional internet charges.
- **Monthly Savings**: Subtract the total monthly cost of streaming from your current cable bill to determine your savings.

Feature/Carrier	Plan 1	Plan 2	Plan 3	Notes
Current Cable Bill				
Streaming Service Options				
Internet Service Upgrade				
Total Monthly Cost				
Monthly Savings				
Additional Fees				
Special Offers				

Action Steps:

- Fill in the worksheet with your current expenses and potential streaming costs.
- Evaluate the total cost of streaming options versus your current cable bill.

Step 6: Test Streaming Services

Many streaming services offer free trials. Use these trials to test the services with your favorite content and assess the streaming quality.

Action Steps:

- Sign up for free trials with your selected streaming services.
- Note any likes or dislikes regarding content availability, user interface, and streaming quality.

Step 7: Make the Switch

If you're satisfied with the streaming options and potential savings, proceed with canceling your cable service.

Action Steps:

- Contact your cable provider to cancel your service. Be prepared for retention offers.
- Officially subscribe to your chosen streaming services.
- Update your cost analysis worksheet to reflect your new monthly entertainment expenses.

Conclusion

Cutting the cord and switching to streaming services can offer not only cost savings but also a viewing experience tailored to your preferences. By following these steps and using the cost analysis worksheet, you'll be equipped to make an informed decision that aligns with your entertainment needs and budget. Remember, the flexibility of streaming services allows you to adjust your subscriptions as your viewing habits change, further optimizing your expenses over time.

4.3 Cutting the Cord: Alternatives to Traditional Cable

In recent years, the shift from traditional cable TV to streaming services has gained significant momentum. "Cutting the cord" refers to canceling cable or satellite subscriptions in favor of internet-based streaming options. This approach can offer more flexibility and often, substantial savings. This guide provides a step-by-step plan for evaluating alternatives to cable, including an options guide and a cost analysis worksheet to help you make an informed decision.

Step 1: Evaluate Your Viewing Habits

Before making any changes, assess your current viewing habits and what you value most in a television service.

Action Steps:

- List your must-have channels, shows, and the type of content you enjoy.
- Note how often you watch live TV versus on-demand content.

Step 2: Research Streaming Services

Explore the wide range of streaming services available, noting which ones offer the content you enjoy.

Action Steps:

- Compile a list of streaming services, such as Netflix, Hulu, Amazon Prime Video, Disney+, and specialized platforms like HBO Max or ESPN+.
- For each service, list the available content, monthly cost, and any additional features like offline viewing or multiple simultaneous streams.

Step 3: Consider Live TV Streaming Options

If live TV is important to you, look into live TV streaming services as a direct replacement for cable.

Action Steps:

- Identify live TV streaming services such as YouTube TV, Sling TV, and Hulu + Live TV.
- Check their channel lineups, pricing, and any restrictions like DVR capabilities or simultaneous streams.

Step 4: Assess Internet Requirements

Streaming quality video requires a reliable and fast internet connection. Ensure your current internet service meets these needs.

Action Steps:

- Determine the internet speed required for high-quality streaming (at least 25 Mbps for 4K streaming).
- If necessary, research options to upgrade your internet service, considering the added cost against potential cable savings.

Step 5: Use a Cost Analysis Worksheet

To compare the costs of streaming services versus traditional cable, utilize a cost analysis worksheet. This tool will help you visualize potential savings.

Cost Analysis Worksheet Components:

- **Current Cable Bill**: Include monthly rate, rental fees, and any additional costs.
- **Streaming Service Options**: List each service you're considering, along with the monthly cost.
- **Internet Service Upgrade (if needed)**: Include the cost of upgrading your internet service.
- **Total Monthly Cost**: Calculate the total cost of streaming services and any additional internet charges.
- **Monthly Savings**: Subtract the total monthly cost of streaming from your current cable bill to determine your savings.

Action Steps:

- Fill in the worksheet with your current expenses and potential streaming costs.
- Evaluate the total cost of streaming options versus your current cable bill.

Step 6: Test Streaming Services

Many streaming services offer free trials. Use these trials to test the services with your favorite content and assess the streaming quality.

Action Steps:

- Sign up for free trials with your selected streaming services.
- Note any likes or dislikes regarding content availability, user interface, and streaming quality.

Step 7: Make the Switch

If you're satisfied with the streaming options and potential savings, proceed with canceling your cable service.

Action Steps:

- Contact your cable provider to cancel your service. Be prepared for retention offers.
- Officially subscribe to your chosen streaming services.
- Update your cost analysis worksheet to reflect your new monthly entertainment expenses.

Conclusion

Cutting the cord and switching to streaming services can offer not only cost savings but also a viewing experience tailored to your preferences. By following these steps and using the cost analysis worksheet, you'll be equipped to make an informed decision that aligns with your entertainment needs and budget. Remember, the flexibility of streaming services allows you to adjust your subscriptions as your viewing habits change, further optimizing your expenses over time.

Chapter 5: Managing Subscriptions and Memberships

5.1 Evaluating Your Subscriptions

Subscriptions can slowly accumulate, often without notice, leading to unnecessary monthly expenses. Regularly evaluating your subscriptions helps you identify which services you truly use and enjoy versus those you can do without.

This process can free up significant funds in your budget. This guide outlines a methodical approach to assess your subscriptions, featuring an inventory worksheet and a cancellation guide to streamline the process.

Step 1: Gather Information on All Subscriptions

Start by compiling a comprehensive list of every subscription service you're currently paying for, including digital streaming, magazines, apps, fitness platforms, and any others.

Action Steps:

- Review your bank statements, credit card statements, and PayPal account for recurring subscription charges over the past year.
- List each subscription in a document or spreadsheet, noting the service name, monthly cost, billing cycle, and the last time you used the service.

Step 2: Assess Usage and Value

Evaluate how often you use each subscription and the value it brings to your life. This will help you determine which subscriptions are worth keeping.

Action Steps:

- Mark each subscription as "Frequently Used," "Sometimes Used," or "Rarely Used" based on your actual usage.
- Reflect on the personal value or enjoyment each service provides.

Step 3: Create an Inventory Worksheet

Organize the collected information into an inventory worksheet. This worksheet will serve as a visual aid to assess your subscriptions collectively.

Subscription Inventory Worksheet Template:

Subscription Name	Monthly Cost	Billing Cycle	Last Used	Usage Frequency	Keep/Cancel
Example:					
Netflix	$15.99	Monthly	This week	Frequently Used	Keep
Gym	$29.99	Monthly	3 months ago	Rarely Used	Cancel

Action Steps:

- Populate the worksheet with the details of each subscription.
- Decide whether to "Keep" or "Cancel" based on your usage and value assessment.

Step 4: Prioritize Cancellations

Identify subscriptions you're ready to cancel. Prioritize these based on potential savings and least usage.

Action Steps:

- Highlight or flag subscriptions marked for cancellation.
- Rank them in order of cancellation priority, considering both financial savings and how infrequently you use the service.

Step 5: Cancel Unwanted Subscriptions

Begin the process of cancelling each subscription you've identified as unnecessary. Be prepared for companies to offer deals or pauses to keep you as a customer.

Cancellation Guide:

- **Locate Cancellation Procedures:** Review the service's terms of service or FAQ section for cancellation instructions.
- **Contact Customer Service:** If needed, call or chat with customer service to cancel. Be firm but polite in your request.
- **Confirm Cancellation:** Ensure you receive a confirmation email or message stating your subscription has been canceled.

Action Steps:

- Systematically work through your list, canceling each subscription and noting the date of cancellation in your worksheet.
- Check your bank or credit card statements in the following months to ensure no further charges are made.

Step 6: Reassess Regularly

Make subscription evaluation a regular part of your financial routine. Set a reminder to review your subscription inventory worksheet periodically.

Action Steps:

- Schedule a semi-annual or annual review of your subscriptions.
- Update your inventory worksheet with any new subscriptions and repeat the assessment process.

Conclusion

Evaluating your subscriptions with a critical eye can lead to significant savings and ensure your monthly spending aligns with your actual needs and values. By following these steps, creating a subscription inventory worksheet, and using the cancellation guide, you'll gain control over your recurring expenses, allowing you to invest or spend your money more wisely elsewhere. Remember, the key to financial well-being is not just in earning more, but in spending smarter.

5.2 Strategies for Managing Subscription Services

In a world increasingly driven by subscription models—from streaming platforms and software to fitness classes and meal kits—keeping track of and optimizing these recurring expenses is crucial for financial health. This guide provides actionable strategies to manage your subscription services effectively, including the use of an optimization worksheet to streamline your expenses.

Step 1: Conduct a Subscription Audit

Begin by identifying all your current subscriptions. This includes everything from digital streaming services and online publications to gym memberships and monthly subscription boxes.

Action Steps:

- Gather bank statements, credit card statements, and email receipts from the past year.
- Create a list (or use an app designed for tracking subscriptions) to note each service, the monthly or annual cost, and the renewal date.

Step 2: Evaluate the Value and Usage of Each Subscription

For each subscription, assess how often you use the service and whether it provides value relative to its cost.

Action Steps:

- Mark each subscription as "Frequently Used," "Occasionally Used," or "Rarely Used."
- Consider the enjoyment or utility derived from each service. Is it worth the cost?

Step 3: Identify Redundancies and Opportunities for Consolidation

Look for overlapping services or those that offer similar content or features, where you might consolidate to a single subscription to save money.

Action Steps:

- Highlight any subscriptions that offer similar services or content.
- Decide which service(s) to keep based on your preference, cost, and usage.

Step 4: Optimize Subscription Costs

Explore ways to reduce the costs of the subscriptions you decide to keep. This might include switching to annual billing for discounts, sharing plans with family or friends, or downgrading to a cheaper plan.

Action Steps:

- Contact customer service to inquire about any available discounts or lower-priced plans.
- Research family or shared plans and coordinate with friends or family members to share costs.

Step 5: Use the Optimization Worksheet

To systematically review and make decisions about your subscriptions, use an optimization worksheet.

Optimization Worksheet Components:

- **Subscription Name**: List each service you're currently subscribed to.
- **Cost (Monthly/Annual)**: Note the cost for easier comparison.
- **Usage Frequency**: Mark as "Frequently," "Occasionally," or "Rarely."
- **Redundant With**: If applicable, list any services it overlaps with.

- **Action Needed**: Include actions such as "Cancel," "Keep," "Downgrade," or "Consolidate."
- **Projected Savings**: Estimate your savings over a month or year by making these changes.

Action Steps:

- Fill in the worksheet based on your audit and evaluation.
- Calculate your total potential savings by optimizing your subscriptions.

Step 6: Take Action

Based on your decisions in the optimization worksheet, proceed to cancel, downgrade, or consolidate your subscriptions.

Action Steps:

- For cancellations, ensure you understand the process for each service, as some may require a phone call or written notice.
- Execute the required actions for each subscription as noted in your worksheet.

Step 7: Monitor and Adjust

After optimizing your subscriptions, monitor your spending and usage to ensure these changes meet your needs and adjust as necessary.

Action Steps:

- Set a reminder to review your subscriptions and usage patterns every few months.
- Be mindful of new subscriptions, and add them to your optimization worksheet to assess their value and impact on your budget.

Conclusion

Effectively managing subscription services can significantly impact your monthly expenditures and overall financial well-being. By conducting a thorough audit, evaluating the value and usage, and taking targeted actions to optimize your subscriptions, you can streamline your expenses and ensure you're only paying for services that truly benefit you. Using the provided optimization worksheet as a tool, you can make informed decisions and adjust your subscription portfolio to better align with your financial goals and lifestyle preferences.

5.3 **When to Bundle Services for Savings**

Bundling services—such as internet, cable, and phone—can lead to significant savings and convenience. However, deciding when and how to bundle requires a thoughtful analysis of your needs, usage, and the offers available in your area. This guide will provide a step-by-step approach to evaluating bundling opportunities, including a bundling worksheet to help you compare your options and make informed decisions.

Step 1: Identify Your Service Needs

The first step in considering a bundle is to clearly understand your needs for each service you're considering bundling. This might include internet, cable TV, home phone, mobile services, or streaming subscriptions.

Action Steps:

- List the services you currently use and those you're considering.
- For each service, note your must-have features or specifications (e.g., internet speed, cable channels, mobile data).

Step 2: Research Bundle Offers

Once you have a clear understanding of your needs, research the bundle offers available from service providers in your area. Pay close attention to the details of each offer, including any promotional terms.

Action Steps:

- Visit the websites of service providers or call their customer service for information on current bundle offers.
- Collect information on the costs, terms, and what's included in each bundle.

Step 3: Analyze Individual vs. Bundle Costs

To determine whether bundling offers genuine savings, compare the cost of subscribing to services individually versus as part of a bundle.

Action Steps:

- List the current or potential individual costs of each service you're considering.
- Compare these costs to the total cost of each bundle option.

Step 4: Use the Bundling Worksheet

A bundling worksheet can help you organize and compare your options systematically.

Bundling Worksheet Components:

- **Service Needed**: List each service you're considering for the bundle.
- **Individual Cost**: Note the cost if subscribed to individually.
- **Bundle Offers**: List the details of each bundle offer you're considering.
- **Total Bundle Cost**: The monthly or annual cost of the bundle.
- **Savings**: Calculate the difference between individual costs and the bundle cost.
- **Pros and Cons**: Note any additional benefits or drawbacks of each option (e.g., contract terms, promotional periods).

Action Steps:

- Fill out the worksheet with the information you've gathered on individual and bundle costs.
- Calculate your potential savings for each bundle option.

Step 5: Consider the Long-Term

Many bundles come with promotional pricing that can change after a certain period. Understanding these terms is crucial to ensuring long-term savings.

Action Steps:

- Note the duration of any promotional pricing and the regular rate post-promotion.
- Calculate the average monthly cost over a longer period (e.g., two years) to assess the true value of the bundle.

Step 6: Evaluate Flexibility and Convenience

Beyond cost savings, consider the added value of convenience and flexibility that bundling might offer, such as a single bill for multiple services or improved customer service experiences.

Action Steps:

- Assess the importance of convenience in managing your services.
- Consider any potential downsides, such as difficulties in changing or canceling services in the future.

Step 7: Make an Informed Decision

Using the insights gained from your analysis and the bundling worksheet, decide whether a bundle offer meets your needs and offers genuine savings and benefits.

Action Steps:

- Review your completed bundling worksheet to compare your options.
- Choose the best bundle option based on your analysis or decide to keep services separate based on your findings.

Conclusion

Determining when to bundle services requires a careful analysis of your needs, usage, and the offers available. By following these steps and utilizing the bundling worksheet, you can make an informed decision that potentially saves money and simplifies your service management.

Remember, the best choice varies by individual needs and market offers, so taking the time to evaluate your options thoroughly is key to finding the most beneficial and cost-effective solution for you.

Chapter 6: Saving on Insurance Premiums

6.1 Shopping for Insurance

Navigating the insurance market to find the right coverage for your needs and budget can be a daunting task. Whether it's health, auto, home, or life insurance, the key to making an informed decision lies in understanding your options and comparing them effectively. This guide outlines a systematic approach to shopping for insurance, including a comparison chart and checklist to ensure you get the best possible deal.

Step 1: Assess Your Insurance Needs

Before diving into the insurance market, it's crucial to evaluate what kind of coverage you need. This depends on various factors, including your lifestyle, financial situation, and any existing coverage you may have.

Action Steps:

- List the types of insurance you are shopping for (e.g., health, auto, home, life).
- For each type, outline your coverage needs, including any specific requirements (such as coverage for chronic conditions, high-value home contents, or specific life insurance beneficiaries).

Step 2: Gather Information on Potential Insurers

Research potential insurance providers, focusing on their reputation, financial stability, customer service, and range of products.

Action Steps:

- Use online reviews, consumer reports, and financial rating agencies like A.M. Best or Moody's to gather information on insurers.
- Create a preliminary list of insurers that meet your criteria.

Step 3: Request Quotes

With your needs in hand, start requesting quotes from the insurers on your list. Make sure to provide consistent information to each insurer to ensure the quotes are comparable.

Action Steps:

- Contact each insurer directly or use online quote comparison tools.
- Keep detailed notes on the coverage options provided and the associated premiums, deductibles, and any exclusions or limitations.

Step 4: Use a Comparison Chart

To effectively compare the insurance quotes and coverage options you've gathered, create a comparison chart.

Comparison Chart Template:

Insurer	Premium	Deductible	Coverage Limits	Exclusions	Customer Service Rating	Notes

Action Steps:

- Fill in the chart with the details of each quote.
- Highlight any differences in coverage, costs, or customer service ratings that are important to you.

Step 5: Check for Discounts and Bundling Options

Many insurers offer discounts for bundling multiple policies or for customers who meet certain criteria (e.g., safe drivers, non-smokers).

Action Steps:

- Inquire about any available discounts or bundling options that could reduce your premiums.
- Update your comparison chart with the discounted premiums for a more accurate comparison.

Step 6: Evaluate the Insurer's Customer Service and Claims Process

The quality of customer service and efficiency of the claims process are as important as the cost and coverage.

Action Steps:

- Read customer testimonials and independent reviews focusing on claims processing and customer service experiences.
- Consider the insurer's accessibility (online portals, mobile apps, 24/7 customer support).

Step 7: Make an Informed Decision

Using the insights from your comparison chart and additional research, select the insurance policy that best meets your needs at the most reasonable cost.

Action Steps:

- Review your comparison chart and prioritize your decision based on the factors most important to you (cost, coverage, customer service).
- Contact the chosen insurer to finalize the policy, making sure to read the fine print before signing any contracts.

Conclusion

Shopping for insurance requires diligent research and comparison to ensure you're getting the best coverage for your needs at a fair price. By following this step-by-step guide and utilizing the comparison chart and checklist, you're equipped to make an informed decision. Remember, insurance is a crucial investment in your financial security and peace of mind, so taking the time to choose wisely is paramount.

6.2 Strategies for Lowering Auto Insurance Costs

Auto insurance is a necessary expense for most drivers, but it doesn't have to break the bank. There are several strategies you can employ to lower your auto insurance costs without compromising on coverage. This guide outlines practical tips for reducing your auto insurance premiums and includes a savings worksheet to help you track your progress.

Step 1: Review Your Current Policy

Start by understanding exactly what your current auto insurance policy covers. Look for any coverages that may no longer be necessary or that you might be overpaying for.

Action Steps:

- Obtain a copy of your current insurance policy and review the coverages, deductibles, and limits.
- Consider whether changes in your life, driving habits, or the age of your vehicle might allow you to adjust or drop certain coverages.

Step 2: Shop Around and Compare Quotes

Insurance rates vary widely among providers, so it's essential to shop around and compare quotes to find the best deal.

Action Steps:

- Gather quotes from multiple insurance companies. Make sure to provide the same information to each for an accurate comparison.
- Use online comparison tools to streamline the process.

Step 3: Increase Your Deductibles

Choosing a higher deductible can significantly lower your premiums. However, make sure you choose a deductible amount you can afford in case of a claim.

Action Steps:

- Calculate how much you could save by increasing your deductible.
- Assess your financial situation to determine if you can comfortably handle the higher deductible in the event of an accident.

Step 4: Look for Discounts

Most insurance companies offer a variety of discounts to policyholders who meet certain criteria.

Action Steps:

- Inquire about available discounts such as for safe driving, anti-theft devices, low mileage, good student, or completing a defensive driving course.
- Ensure any discounts you qualify for are applied to your policy.

Step 5: Bundle Insurance Policies

Bundling your auto insurance with other policies, such as homeowners or renters insurance, can lead to substantial savings.

Action Steps:

- Check with your insurance provider about bundling options.
- Compare the bundled price with the total cost of holding policies with separate insurers.

Step 6: Maintain a Good Credit Score

Many insurers use credit information to price auto insurance policies. A better credit score can lead to lower premiums.

Action Steps:

- Regularly check your credit score and report for any errors.
- Work on improving your credit score through timely payments and reducing debt.

Step 7: Use a Savings Worksheet

A savings worksheet helps you track the potential savings from implementing these strategies.

Savings Worksheet Components:

- **Current Premium**: Your current auto insurance premium.
- **Quoted Premiums**: Premiums quoted by other insurers.
- **Deductible Adjustment**: Savings from increasing your deductible.
- **Discounts**: Potential savings from applicable discounts.
- **Bundle Savings**: Savings from bundling policies.
- **Total Estimated Savings**: The sum of all potential savings.

Action Steps:

- Fill out the worksheet with the information gathered from the above steps.
- Calculate your total potential savings to see how much you could reduce your auto insurance costs.

Conclusion

Lowering your auto insurance premiums doesn't have to mean sacrificing quality coverage. By thoroughly reviewing your current policy, shopping around, taking advantage of discounts, and considering changes to your deductible, you can significantly reduce your costs. Use the tips and savings worksheet provided in this guide to systematically approach lowering your auto insurance costs and ensure you're getting the best possible rate for your needs.

6.3 Saving on Homeowners and Renters Insurance

Homeowners and renters insurance are essential for protecting your home and personal belongings. However, ensuring you're not overpaying requires regular review and understanding of your policy. This guide provides actionable steps for saving on homeowners and renters insurance, including a policy review worksheet to help assess your current coverage and identify potential savings.

Step 1: Understand Your Current Policy

Begin by thoroughly reviewing your existing insurance policy to understand the extent of your coverage, including any deductibles, limits, and exclusions.

Action Steps:

- Request the latest copy of your policy from your insurance provider if you don't already have it.
- Highlight key areas such as coverage types, policy limits, deductible amounts, and any special endorsements or riders.

Step 2: Assess Your Coverage Needs

Evaluate whether your current coverage accurately reflects your needs. Over time, changes in the value of your property or possessions may necessitate adjustments to your policy.

Action Steps:

- Inventory your possessions and estimate their current replacement value.
- Consider any recent improvements to your home that might affect its replacement cost.
- Decide if there are areas where you might be over-insured (coverage exceeds the value of assets) or under-insured (insufficient coverage for the replacement value).

Step 3: Shop Around for Quotes

Insurance rates can vary significantly between providers, even for similar coverage. Shopping around can uncover opportunities to save.

Action Steps:

- Obtain quotes from multiple insurance companies, ensuring you provide the same information to each for comparable quotes.
- Use online comparison tools for a broader view of the market.

Step 4: Look for Discounts

Many insurers offer discounts that can lead to substantial savings on your premium.

Action Steps:

- Inquire about discounts for which you may be eligible, such as security system installations, smoke detectors, bundling policies (auto and home/renters), loyalty discounts, or claims-free history.
- Make sure any applicable discounts are applied to your policy.

Step 5: Consider Increasing Your Deductible

A higher deductible can lower your premium but means paying more out-of-pocket in the event of a claim. Assess your financial readiness to handle a higher deductible.

Action Steps:

- Calculate the difference in premium costs for various deductible amounts.
- Evaluate your emergency fund or savings to determine if you can comfortably afford a higher deductible if necessary.

Step 6: Use the Policy Review Worksheet

A policy review worksheet organizes the information about your current coverage and potential savings opportunities.

Policy Review Worksheet Components:

- **Current Coverage Details**: List your current coverage limits, deductibles, and premium.
- **Coverage Needs Assessment**: Note any changes in coverage needs based on your inventory and property improvements.
- **Competitive Quotes**: Record quotes received from other insurers.
- **Discount Opportunities**: List potential discounts and the savings associated with each.
- **Deductible Analysis**: Compare the impact of different deductible levels on your premium.
- **Decision Notes**: Space to note your decision on adjusting coverage, changing providers, or other actions.

Action Steps:

- Complete the worksheet with the information gathered through the above steps.
- Use the worksheet to evaluate where you can adjust your policy for savings without sacrificing necessary coverage.

Conclusion

Regularly reviewing your homeowners or renters insurance policy is key to ensuring you have adequate coverage at the best possible price. By understanding your current policy, assessing your coverage needs, shopping around, taking advantage of discounts, and considering a higher deductible, you can identify opportunities to save on your premium.

Chapter 7: Food and Grocery Savings

7.1 Effective Meal Planning and Budgeting

Effective meal planning and budgeting are key strategies for reducing grocery bills, minimizing food waste, and eating healthier. This step-by-step guide provides actionable advice on creating a meal plan and budget, accompanied by tools such as a meal planner and budget worksheet to streamline the process.

Step 1: Assess Your Food Spending

Begin by tracking your current spending on groceries, dining out, and snacks to establish a baseline. Understanding where your money is going can highlight areas for improvement.

Action Steps:

- Collect receipts and bank statements from the past month to tally your total food expenditure.
- Categorize spending into groceries, dining out, and miscellaneous food items.

Step 2: Set a Realistic Food Budget

Based on your spending assessment, set a realistic monthly food budget that aligns with your financial goals. Consider areas where you can cut back, especially on dining out and convenience foods.

Action Steps:

- Determine a monthly amount you aim to spend on food, dividing it into weekly budgets for easier management.
- Remember to account for any special occasions or dining out plans.

Step 3: Plan Your Meals

Planning your meals for the week is the cornerstone of effective meal planning and budgeting. This helps in buying only what you need, reducing waste, and avoiding impulse purchases.

Action Steps:

- Use a meal planner tool or template to outline meals for each day, including breakfast, lunch, dinner, and snacks.
- Incorporate meals that use similar ingredients to maximize the use of all purchased items.

Step 4: Create a Shopping List

Based on your meal plan, create a detailed shopping list. This ensures you purchase only necessary items, sticking to your budget and reducing waste.

Action Steps:

- List ingredients needed for your planned meals, checking your pantry and fridge first to avoid buying duplicates.
- Organize your list by store sections (produce, dairy, meats, etc.) for efficiency.

Step 5: Stick to Your List and Shop Smart

When grocery shopping, staying disciplined and sticking to your list are crucial for staying within your budget.

Action Steps:

- Avoid shopping when hungry to prevent impulse buys.
- Consider generic brands, which often offer the same quality as name brands at a lower price.
- Look out for sales on staple items, but only buy what you'll use.

Step 6: Use the Budget Worksheet

A budget worksheet helps track your spending against your budget, ensuring you stay on track throughout the month.

Budget Worksheet Components:

- **Budgeted Amount**: Your total monthly food budget.
- **Weekly Spending**: Record what you spend each week on groceries and dining out.
- **Over/Under**: Calculate whether you're over or under budget each week.
- **Notes**: Include observations on what worked well or where you can improve.

Action Steps:

- Update your budget worksheet after each shopping trip or meal out.
- Review weekly spending to adjust behaviors or meal plans as necessary.

Step 7: Review and Adjust

At the end of each month, review your meal planning and budgeting efforts. Identify what worked, what didn't, and areas for improvement.

Action Steps:

- Reflect on your meal satisfaction, budget adherence, and any challenges faced.
- Adjust your meal planning and budgeting strategies based on insights gained for continuous improvement.

Conclusion

Effective meal planning and budgeting require commitment and regular adjustment to align with your dietary preferences and financial goals. By diligently following this guide and utilizing the meal planner and budget worksheet, you can make informed decisions that lead to savings, reduced food waste, and healthier eating habits. These practices not only benefit your wallet but also contribute to a sustainable lifestyle.

7.2 Maximizing Savings with Coupons, Discounts, and Cashback Apps

In the quest for financial savvy, leveraging coupons, discounts, and cashback apps can significantly reduce expenses on everyday purchases. This guide provides a step-by-step approach to integrating these savings tools into your shopping routine, complemented by a savings tracker to monitor your success.

Step 1: Identify Reliable Sources for Coupons and Discounts

The first step in harnessing the power of savings is to know where to find the best deals. This includes traditional sources like newspapers and mailers, as well as digital platforms.

Action Steps:

- Subscribe to newsletters from your favorite stores to receive coupons and early notification of sales directly to your inbox.
- Follow brands and retailers on social media for exclusive discounts.
- Download reputable coupon websites and browser extensions that automatically apply the best coupon codes at checkout.

Step 2: Choose Cashback and Rewards Apps

Cashback apps and rewards programs return a portion of your spending back to you. Selecting the right ones can turn everyday purchases into savings.

Action Steps:

- Research and sign up for cashback apps that work with stores where you frequently shop.
- Consider credit cards that offer cashback or rewards points on purchases, if they align with your spending habits and financial discipline.

Step 3: Develop a Routine for Checking Deals

Incorporating a quick check for coupons, discounts, and cashback opportunities into your shopping routine ensures you never miss out on savings.

Action Steps:

- Before making any purchase, large or small, take a moment to search for applicable coupons or cashback offers.
- Use your selected cashback apps to scan receipts or complete online purchases to ensure you receive your rewards.

Step 4: Combine Savings Strategies

Maximize your savings by combining coupons, sales, and cashback offers. This layered approach can lead to significant discounts.

Action Steps:

- Look for items on sale that you also have coupons for, then complete the purchase through a cashback app or site.
- Be mindful of store policies regarding the use of multiple coupons or combining coupons with sales.

Step 5: Track Your Savings

To truly understand the impact of your efforts, maintain a savings tracker. This tool will help you visualize the amount saved over time.

Savings Tracker Components:

- **Date**: When the purchase was made.
- **Item/Service**: What you bought.
- **Retail Price**: The original price without discounts.
- **Savings from Coupons/Discounts**: The amount saved using coupons or discounts.
- **Cashback Earned**: Any cashback received from apps or rewards programs.
- **Total Savings**: The sum of savings and cashback.
- **Notes**: Any relevant details or strategies used.

Action Steps:

- After each shopping trip or online purchase, update your savings tracker with the relevant details.
- Review your tracker regularly to assess which strategies are most effective and adjust your approach accordingly.

Step 6: Evaluate and Optimize Your Savings Strategy

With data from your savings tracker, analyze which types of deals offer the most savings and which apps or methods yield the best returns.

Action Steps:

- Identify patterns in your savings, such as particular stores or types of products where you save the most.
- Adjust your shopping habits to focus on strategies that maximize savings, such as shopping at stores with the best cashback rates or stocking up on items during major sales.

Conclusion

Effectively using coupons, discounts, and cashback apps requires a bit of effort and organization but can lead to substantial savings. By following this guide and diligently updating your savings tracker, you'll not only save money but also gain a deeper understanding of your spending habits, empowering you to make more informed financial decisions. The key to success lies in the routine you develop and the insights you glean from tracking your savings over time.

7.3 The Benefits of Bulk Buying

Bulk buying can be a powerful strategy to save money on groceries, household items, and other products you use regularly. By purchasing items in larger quantities, you can take advantage of lower unit prices, reduce the frequency of shopping trips, and ensure you always have essential items on hand. However, it's important to approach bulk buying strategically to maximize benefits and avoid wastage. This guide provides actionable steps to implement bulk buying into your shopping habits, including a savings calculator to help you quantify your savings.

Step 1: Assess Your Storage Space

Before you start bulk buying, assess how much storage space you have available. This will help you avoid purchasing more than you can store.

Action Steps:

- Evaluate your pantry, freezer, and storage areas to determine how much space you have for bulk items.
- Consider organizing or decluttering to maximize storage efficiency.

Step 2: Identify Items Suitable for Bulk Buying

Not all items are suitable for bulk purchases. Focus on non-perishable goods, items you use frequently, and products that won't go bad before you can use them.

Action Steps:

- Make a list of non-perishable goods you regularly use (e.g., rice, pasta, canned goods).
- Include household items like toilet paper, detergent, and personal care products.

Step 3: Compare Prices and Calculate Potential Savings

To ensure bulk buying actually saves you money, compare unit prices and calculate the potential savings over buying smaller quantities.

Action Steps:

- Use the unit price (price per ounce, liter, pound, etc.) to compare bulk items with regular-sized items.
- Record the prices and sizes of items in a savings calculator spreadsheet.

Step 4: Use a Savings Calculator

A savings calculator can help you clearly see the financial benefits of bulk buying.

Savings Calculator Components:

- **Item Name**: The product you're considering buying in bulk.
- **Bulk Price**: The cost of the item in bulk.
- **Regular Price**: The cost of the item in regular size.
- **Unit Price Bulk**: The unit price of the bulk item.
- **Unit Price Regular**: The unit price of the regular-sized item.
- **Quantity Needed**: How much of the item you typically use.
- **Savings**: The difference in cost over a set period of using the bulk vs. regular size.

Action Steps:

- Fill out the calculator with the items you're considering for bulk purchase.
- Use the data to identify which items offer the most significant savings when bought in bulk.

Step 5: Make a Shopping List and Stick to It

To avoid impulsive buys, make a detailed shopping list based on your savings calculator and storage capacity.

Action Steps:

- List the items you've identified as cost-effective to buy in bulk.
- Stick to your list when shopping to avoid unnecessary purchases.

Step 6: Monitor Consumption and Adjust Purchases

Track how quickly you go through bulk items to adjust your purchasing habits accordingly. This helps prevent overbuying and wastage.

Action Steps:

- Note how long it takes to use up bulk-purchased items.
- Adjust your future bulk purchases based on consumption rates to avoid excess.

Step 7: Review and Optimize Your Bulk Buying Strategy

Periodically review your bulk buying habits, savings, and consumption patterns to refine your strategy.

Action Steps:

- Use your savings calculator to assess the financial benefits of your bulk purchases.
- Consider any changes in storage space, consumption habits, or product availability that might affect your bulk buying strategy.

Conclusion

Bulk buying, when done strategically, can lead to significant savings and convenience. By assessing your storage space, carefully selecting suitable items, comparing prices, and calculating potential savings, you can make informed decisions that positively impact your budget.

The savings calculator is an invaluable tool for visualizing the benefits and guiding your purchases. Remember, the goal of bulk buying is to save money without sacrificing quality or leading to wastage, so continually adjust your strategy based on your actual needs and experiences.

Chapter 8: Transportation and Fuel Savings

8.1 Economical Commuting Options

Exploring economical commuting options can significantly reduce your monthly transportation expenses and contribute to environmental conservation. Whether it's carpooling, public transportation, biking, or walking, choosing the right commuting method can have a profound impact on your budget and well-being. This guide provides actionable steps to assess and implement the most cost-effective commuting strategies, supplemented by a comparison chart and savings worksheet to help you make an informed decision.

Step 1: Assess Your Current Commuting Costs

Understanding your current commuting costs is crucial to identifying potential savings. Consider all expenses associated with your commute, including fuel, parking fees, vehicle maintenance, or public transit fares.

Action Steps:

- Track your commuting expenses for a typical month, including gas, parking, tolls, and any public transit costs.
- Summarize these costs to establish your current monthly commuting expenditure.

Step 2: Identify Available Commuting Options

Research the commuting options available to you, such as public transportation routes, carpooling networks, bike paths, and walkable routes.

Action Steps:

- Gather information on public transit routes, schedules, and fares.
- Investigate carpooling options, including colleagues who live nearby or carpool matching services.
- Assess the feasibility of biking or walking to work, considering distance, safety, and infrastructure.

Step 3: Use a Commuting Comparison Chart

A comparison chart allows you to evaluate the pros and cons, as well as the costs, of each commuting option side by side.

Commuting Comparison Chart Components:

- **Commuting Option**: List each potential commuting method.
- **Monthly Cost**: Estimate the monthly cost associated with each option.
- **Time**: Note the average commute time for each method.
- **Pros and Cons**: Include benefits such as exercise or drawbacks like weather dependence.
- **Environmental Impact**: Consider the eco-friendliness of each option.

Action Steps:

- Complete the chart with data collected for each commuting option.
- Evaluate which options are the most cost-effective, time-efficient, and environmentally friendly.

Step 4: Implement Economical Commuting Strategies

Based on your comparison chart, choose the commuting option(s) that offer the best balance of cost savings, convenience, and environmental benefits.

Action Steps:

- Prepare for your new commuting method, whether it's purchasing a transit pass, arranging a carpool schedule, or getting your bike ready for regular use.
- Trial your chosen commuting option for at least a month to accurately assess its impact.

Step 5: Use the Savings Worksheet

A savings worksheet helps you track the financial impact of switching to a more economical commuting method.

Savings Worksheet Components:

- **Commuting Method**: The alternative commuting option you're using.
- **Initial Costs**: Any upfront costs incurred (e.g., bike purchase, transit pass).
- **Monthly Commuting Cost Before**: Your original commuting costs.
- **Monthly Commuting Cost After**: Costs associated with the new commuting method.
- **Monthly Savings**: The difference between before and after costs.
- **Annual Savings**: Total savings over a year.

Action Steps:

- Fill in the worksheet with your commuting costs before and after the change.
- Calculate your monthly and annual savings to quantify the benefits of switching commuting methods.

Step 6: Review and Adjust

Regularly review your commuting strategy to ensure it continues to meet your needs and maximize savings.

Action Steps:

- Periodically re-evaluate your commuting costs and options, especially if your circumstances change (e.g., moving to a new home, changes in public transit services).
- Consider exploring additional options or combining methods (e.g., biking to a transit station) for further savings and convenience.

Conclusion

Choosing the right commuting option can lead to substantial savings and a lower environmental footprint. By assessing your current costs, comparing alternatives, and tracking your savings, you can make an informed decision that enhances your financial well-being and supports a sustainable lifestyle.

Remember, the most economical commuting method for you will depend on your unique situation, including distance, available options, and personal preferences. Regularly revisiting your commuting strategy ensures that you continue to commute in the most efficient and cost-effective manner possible.

8.2 Saving on Vehicle Maintenance and Fuel

Proper vehicle maintenance and fuel efficiency practices are essential for prolonging the life of your vehicle, enhancing safety, and reducing overall costs. This guide outlines actionable steps to save on vehicle maintenance and fuel, incorporating a maintenance schedule and cost tracker to help you manage expenses effectively.

Step 1: Understand Your Vehicle's Maintenance Needs

Begin by familiarizing yourself with your vehicle's maintenance requirements, which are crucial for keeping it in optimal condition and avoiding costly repairs down the line.

Action Steps:

- Consult your vehicle's owner manual to understand recommended maintenance intervals for oil changes, tire rotations, brake inspections, and other services.
- Make a list of upcoming maintenance tasks based on the vehicle's current mileage and manufacturer's recommendations.

Step 2: Create a Maintenance Schedule

A well-planned maintenance schedule ensures you stay on top of necessary vehicle upkeep tasks, preventing minor issues from turning into major expenses.

Maintenance Schedule Components:

- **Maintenance Task**: List each service required (e.g., oil change, tire rotation).
- **Frequency/Interval**: Specify how often or at what mileage intervals each task should be performed.
- **Next Due Date/Mileage**: Note when or at what mileage the next service is due.
- **Estimated Cost**: Research and note the average cost for each maintenance task.

Action Steps:

- Fill out the maintenance schedule according to your vehicle's maintenance guide and current mileage.
- Set reminders for upcoming maintenance tasks to ensure they are not overlooked.

Step 3: Shop Around for Maintenance Services

Costs for vehicle maintenance services can vary significantly between providers. Shopping around and looking for reputable service centers can lead to substantial savings.

Action Steps:

- Obtain quotes from multiple service centers for the maintenance tasks you need.
- Check reviews and ratings to ensure the quality of service is not compromised for a lower price.

Step 4: Implement Fuel-Saving Practices

Adopting fuel-efficient driving habits can significantly reduce your vehicle's fuel consumption, lowering ongoing operational costs.

Action Steps:

- Practice smooth driving techniques, avoiding rapid acceleration and hard braking.
- Maintain a steady speed on highways, and use cruise control when appropriate.
- Ensure your tires are properly inflated to the pressure recommended by the vehicle manufacturer.
- Remove unnecessary weight from the vehicle and minimize the use of roof racks to reduce drag.

Step 5: Use a Cost Tracker

A cost tracker helps you monitor your spending on maintenance and fuel, providing insights into how your actions impact overall vehicle costs.

Cost Tracker Components:

- **Date**: When the maintenance service was performed or fuel was purchased.
- **Description**: A brief description of the service or noting it as a fuel purchase.
- **Cost**: The amount spent on the service or fuel.
- **Mileage**: The vehicle's mileage at the time of service or fuel purchase.
- **Notes**: Any observations or additional information relevant to the service or fuel efficiency.

Action Steps:

- Update the cost tracker each time you complete a maintenance service or fill up your tank.
- Review the tracker periodically to assess where savings are being made and where further improvements can be implemented.

Step 6: Regularly Review and Adjust Your Maintenance and Fuel Practices

Continuously evaluate your vehicle's maintenance and fuel consumption patterns. Adjust your driving habits and maintenance practices as needed to maximize savings.

Action Steps:

- Analyze the data from your cost tracker to identify trends or areas for improvement.
- Consider additional fuel-saving modifications or maintenance practices that could further reduce costs.

Conclusion

Effective vehicle maintenance and adopting fuel-efficient driving habits are key strategies for minimizing vehicle-related expenses. By creating a maintenance schedule, shopping around for maintenance services, practicing fuel-saving techniques, and tracking your costs, you can significantly reduce the financial burden of owning and operating a vehicle. Regular reviews and adjustments to your approach will ensure you continue to achieve optimal savings over the life of your vehicle.

8.3 The Advantages of Carpooling and Public Transportation

Carpooling and using public transportation are not only eco-friendly choices but can also significantly reduce commuting costs compared to driving solo. This guide will provide actionable steps to leverage these options effectively, along with a comprehensive expense comparison worksheet to help you visualize potential savings.

Step 1: Evaluate Your Commuting Needs

Understanding your daily commuting needs is crucial for determining whether carpooling, public transportation, or a combination of both is the most efficient option for you.

Action Steps:

- Note your daily commute distance, preferred travel times, and any flexibility in your schedule.
- Consider any additional commuting needs, such as errands or activities.

Step 2: Research Public Transportation Options

Investigate the public transportation services available in your area, including routes, schedules, and costs. Many cities offer a variety of options, including buses, trains, and subways.

Action Steps:

- Visit the website of your local public transportation agency for route maps and schedules.
- Calculate the monthly cost of using public transportation based on daily fares or the availability of monthly passes.

Step 3: Explore Carpooling Opportunities

Carpooling can be an effective way to reduce commuting costs and contribute to reducing traffic congestion and pollution.

Action Steps:

- Use carpooling apps or websites, or check with your workplace for carpooling programs to find potential matches in your area.
- Discuss schedules, pick-up points, and cost-sharing arrangements with potential carpool partners.

Step 4: Use the Expense Comparison Worksheet

To objectively assess the financial benefits of carpooling and public transportation, use an expense comparison worksheet.

Expense Comparison Worksheet Components:

- **Commuting Option**: List driving solo, carpooling, and public transportation.
- **Monthly Fuel/Transport Costs**: Estimate the cost of fuel for driving solo and share for carpooling, or the fare for public transportation.
- **Parking Fees**: Include monthly parking costs for driving solo or carpooling.
- **Vehicle Maintenance**: Estimate the monthly cost of wear and tear on your vehicle for driving solo compared to reduced use when carpooling.
- **Total Monthly Cost**: Sum the costs for each option.
- **Annual Savings**: Calculate the annual savings of each option

Action Steps:

- Fill in each section of the worksheet with your estimated costs.
- Review the total monthly and annual costs to see which option offers the greatest savings.

Step 5: Implement Your Chosen Commuting Strategy

Based on your findings from the expense comparison worksheet, choose the most cost-effective and convenient commuting option.

Action Steps:

- If choosing public transportation, purchase any necessary passes and familiarize yourself with timetables and routes.
- If carpooling, finalize arrangements with your carpool group, including schedules, routes, and payment methods.

Step 6: Monitor Your Commuting Costs and Adjust as Needed

Keep track of your actual commuting expenses to ensure they align with your estimates and to identify any opportunities for further savings.

Action Steps:

- Regularly update your expense comparison worksheet with actual commuting costs.
- Be flexible and willing to adjust your commuting strategy if you identify a more efficient or cost-effective option.

Conclusion

Switching to carpooling or public transportation can offer significant savings over driving solo, along with environmental benefits. By carefully evaluating your commuting needs, researching available options, and using the expense comparison worksheet to guide your decision, you can select a commuting strategy that optimizes both your budget and time. Regularly revisiting your choice and costs ensures that you continue to commute in the most effective way possible.

Chapter 9: Advanced Saving Strategies

9.1 Tax Strategies for Maximizing Deductions

Maximizing your tax deductions can significantly reduce your taxable income and lower your tax bill. Understanding and leveraging eligible deductions requires careful planning and organization. This guide outlines strategic steps for identifying potential deductions and includes a checklist and deductions worksheet to help you organize and track these tax-saving opportunities.

Step 1: Familiarize Yourself with Common Deductions

Begin by educating yourself on the various deductions that taxpayers often qualify for. These can range from work-related expenses to educational costs, charitable contributions, and health care expenses.

Action Steps:

- Review the IRS website or consult with a tax professional to learn about common deductions.
- Note any deductions that may apply to your situation based on your employment, lifestyle, and any significant expenses incurred during the year.

Step 2: Keep Detailed Records

Maintaining thorough records of potentially deductible expenses throughout the year is crucial for maximizing your deductions.

Action Steps:

- Organize receipts, bills, and statements related to deductible expenses in a dedicated filing system, whether digital or physical.
- Track mileage for work-related trips, medical appointments, or charitable activities if applicable.

Step 3: Utilize a Checklist for Potential Deductions

A checklist helps ensure you don't overlook any opportunities for deductions. Tailor your checklist to your personal and financial situation.

Deductions Checklist Components:

- **Charitable Donations**: Cash and non-cash contributions to qualified organizations.
- **Educational Expenses**: Tuition, fees, and required materials for education that improves job skills.
- **Medical and Dental Expenses**: Costs not covered by insurance, exceeding a certain percentage of your adjusted gross income (AGI).
- **Work-Related Expenses**: Unreimbursed expenses related to your job.
- **Home Office Deduction**: If you're self-employed and use part of your home regularly and exclusively for business.
- **Retirement Contributions**: Contributions to IRAs or self-employed retirement plans.
- **State and Local Taxes (SALT)**: Property taxes and either state income or sales taxes up to a certain limit.

Action Steps:

- Regularly update your checklist as you incur relevant expenses.
- Consult the IRS guidelines or a tax professional to ensure accuracy and compliance.

Step 4: Complete a Deductions Worksheet

A deductions worksheet helps quantify your eligible deductions and provides a clear overview of your potential tax savings.

Deductions Worksheet Components:

- **Category**: List each category of deductions identified in your checklist.
- **Estimated Amount**: Document the estimated amount for each deduction based on your records.
- **Supporting Documentation**: Note the type of documentation you have for each deduction (receipts, bank statements, mileage logs, etc.).
- **Eligibility Notes**: Include any specific conditions or limits related to the deduction.

Action Steps:

- Fill in the worksheet throughout the year as you gather documentation for your deductions.
- Review and update the worksheet in preparation for tax filing.

Step 5: Review and Optimize Your Tax Situation

Before filing your taxes, review your deductions worksheet and checklist to identify any additional tax planning opportunities or areas needing clarification.

Action Steps:

- Consider consulting a tax professional to review your worksheet and ensure you're maximizing your deductions.
- Investigate whether taking the standard deduction or itemizing your deductions is more beneficial based on your compiled information.

Conclusion

Implementing tax strategies to maximize deductions requires year-round attention and organization. By familiarizing yourself with eligible deductions, maintaining detailed records, utilizing a checklist, and completing a deductions worksheet, you can effectively reduce your taxable income and lower your overall tax liability. Regular review and consultation with a tax professional can further enhance your tax-saving efforts, ensuring you take full advantage of available deductions while complying with tax laws.

9.2 Investing in Energy-Efficient Home Improvements

Investing in energy-efficient home improvements can significantly reduce your utility bills and increase your property's value. While upfront costs can be a concern, the long-term savings and environmental benefits make these investments worthwhile. This guide outlines steps to identify and implement energy-efficient upgrades, accompanied by an ROI (Return on Investment) calculator to help you evaluate the financial benefits.

Step 1: Conduct an Energy Audit

An energy audit helps identify areas where your home is losing energy and what improvements can make it more efficient.

Action Steps:

- Hire a professional energy auditor to assess your home or use online tools provided by utility companies for a basic assessment.
- Focus on areas like insulation, windows, doors, and heating and cooling systems.

Step 2: Prioritize High-Impact Improvements

Based on the energy audit, prioritize improvements that offer the most significant energy savings and return on investment.

Action Steps:

- Identify improvements with immediate impact, such as sealing leaks and adding insulation.
- Consider larger projects like upgrading to energy-efficient HVAC systems, windows, or solar panels, based on their potential for long-term savings.

Step 3: Research Incentives and Rebates

Many governments and utility companies offer incentives, rebates, or tax credits for energy-efficient home improvements.

Action Steps:

- Research available incentives in your area through government websites or your utility provider.
- Calculate how these incentives can offset the initial costs of your improvements.

Step 4: Use the ROI Calculator

An ROI calculator can help you estimate the financial return of your energy-efficient investments over time.

ROI Calculator Components:

- **Improvement Cost**: The upfront cost of each energy-efficient upgrade.
- **Annual Energy Savings**: Estimated annual savings on your energy bills resulting from each improvement.
- **Incentives/Rebates**: Any available incentives or rebates that reduce the initial cost.
- **Net Cost**: The improvement cost minus incentives/rebates.
- **ROI**: The return on investment, calculated by dividing the annual energy savings by the net cost.

Action Steps:

- Input the cost and estimated energy savings for each planned improvement into the calculator.
- Factor in any incentives or rebates to find the net cost and calculate the ROI.

Step 5: Implement the Improvements

Begin implementing the energy-efficient improvements, starting with those that offer the highest ROI and are most critical based on your energy audit.

Action Steps:

- For DIY projects, purchase materials and follow best practices for installation.
- For larger projects, obtain quotes from several contractors specializing in energy-efficient installations.
- Schedule the improvements, starting with those that can be completed quickly to realize immediate savings.

Step 6: Monitor Your Energy Savings

After completing the improvements, monitor your utility bills to track the actual savings and validate the effectiveness of each upgrade.

Action Steps:

- Compare your energy bills from before and after the improvements to measure savings.
- Adjust your ROI calculations based on actual savings to assess the success of your investments.

Conclusion

Investing in energy-efficient home improvements requires careful planning and analysis, but the benefits of reduced energy bills and increased home value are significant. By conducting an energy audit, prioritizing high-impact improvements, taking advantage of incentives, and using an ROI calculator, homeowners can make informed decisions about which upgrades offer the best financial and environmental returns.

9.3 Generating Additional Income to Offset Expenses

In today's dynamic economic landscape, generating additional income can be a strategic way to offset expenses and enhance financial security. Whether you're looking to cover specific costs, save more, or invest in the future, additional income streams can provide the necessary boost to your budget. This guide outlines a variety of ideas for generating extra income, accompanied by an action plan worksheet to help you implement these strategies effectively.

Ideas for Generating Additional Income

1. **Freelancing**: Utilize your professional skills to offer services on a freelance basis. Platforms like Upwork and Freelancer can connect you with clients in need of your expertise.
2. **Online Tutoring**: If you excel in a particular subject or skill, online tutoring can be a lucrative way to earn extra money.
3. **Selling Products Online**: Platforms like Etsy and eBay make it easy to sell handmade goods, vintage items, or even products sourced from suppliers.
4. **Rental Income**: If you have extra space, consider renting out a room or property on Airbnb or a similar platform.
5. **Investing in Dividend Stocks**: Investing in dividend-paying stocks can provide a steady stream of passive income.
6. **Creating Digital Products**: E-books, courses, and other digital products can be created once and sold repeatedly online.
7. **Affiliate Marketing**: Earn commissions by promoting other companies' products through a blog, YouTube channel, or social media.

Step 1: Assess Your Skills and Resources

Before diving into a new income-generating venture, assess your current skills, interests, and the resources available to you.

Action Steps:

- Make a list of your skills, hobbies, and areas of expertise that could potentially generate income.
- Evaluate the resources you have, such as a spare room, a reliable computer, or crafting supplies.

Step 2: Choose One or Two Ideas to Start

Focusing on too many ideas at once can be overwhelming. Select one or two that align with your skills, interests, and resources.

Action Steps:

- Based on your assessment, choose the idea(s) you're most excited about and that seem most viable.
- Conduct initial research to understand the market demand and potential income.

Step 3: Use the Action Plan Worksheet

An action plan worksheet helps you break down your chosen income-generating idea into actionable steps, timelines, and goals.

Action Plan Worksheet Components:

- **Idea/Project Name**: The income-generating idea you've chosen to pursue.
- **Objective**: Define what success looks like for this project (e.g., earning a specific amount each month).
- **Action Steps**: List specific actions required to launch and maintain your project (e.g., setting up a website, creating product listings).
- **Timeline**: Assign deadlines to each action step to keep yourself on track.
- **Resources Needed**: Identify any resources or investments required (e.g., website hosting, marketing budget).
- **Progress Tracking**: Create a system for monitoring your progress and income generated.

Action Steps:

- Complete the worksheet for your selected income idea, detailing each step required to get started and grow.
- Schedule regular check-ins to assess progress and make adjustments as needed.

Step 4: Launch and Promote Your Project

With your action plan in place, launch your project and focus on promotion to attract customers or clients.

Action Steps:

- Utilize social media, networking, and relevant online platforms to promote your offering.
- Consider creating a marketing plan to reach your target audience effectively.

Step 5: Evaluate and Adjust

As you begin to generate income, regularly evaluate the effectiveness of your approach and be open to making adjustments.

Action Steps:

- Analyze what's working and what isn't in terms of income generation and workload.
- Be flexible in adjusting your strategy, whether that means refining your offering, exploring new marketing channels, or even pivoting to a different income idea if necessary.

Conclusion

Generating additional income requires clarity, planning, and persistence. By leveraging your skills and resources, following a structured action plan, and continuously evaluating your progress, you can successfully create new income streams to offset expenses and achieve your financial goals. Remember, the key to success lies in starting small, learning from the experience, and gradually scaling your efforts based on what works best for you.

Chapter 10: Future-Proofing Your Savings

10.1 Building an Emergency Fund

An emergency fund is a financial safety net designed to cover unexpected expenses or financial downturns without resorting to high-interest debt. Building and maintaining an adequate emergency fund is essential for financial stability. This guide outlines actionable steps to establish your emergency fund, complemented by a savings goal worksheet to help you plan and track your progress.

Step 1: Determine Your Emergency Fund Goal

The first step in building an emergency fund is to determine how much money you need to save. A common recommendation is to aim for 3 to 6 months' worth of living expenses.

Action Steps:

- Calculate your monthly living expenses, including rent or mortgage, utilities, groceries, insurance, and any other recurring payments.
- Decide on your target emergency fund size based on your personal and financial situation (e.g., job stability, family responsibilities).

Step 2: Set a Monthly Savings Goal

With your total emergency fund goal in mind, break it down into manageable monthly savings targets.

Action Steps:

- Based on your budget, determine how much you can realistically save each month towards your emergency fund.
- Consider adjusting your budget to increase savings, such as by reducing discretionary spending.

Step 3: Open a Dedicated Savings Account

Keeping your emergency fund in a separate savings account helps avoid the temptation to spend it and makes it easier to track your progress.

Action Steps:

- Research savings accounts with high interest rates and low fees to maximize your fund's growth and accessibility.
- Open a dedicated account for your emergency fund and set up automatic transfers from your checking account to coincide with your paydays.

Step 4: Use the Savings Goal Worksheet

A savings goal worksheet helps you plan your savings strategy and monitor your progress toward your emergency fund goal.

Savings Goal Worksheet Components:

- **Total Emergency Fund Goal**: The total amount you aim to save.
- **Monthly Savings Goal**: How much you plan to save each month.
- **Current Savings**: The amount already saved in your emergency fund.
- **Monthly Contributions**: Record your actual monthly contributions.
- **Remaining Balance**: The amount still needed to reach your goal.

Action Steps:

- Fill in your total emergency fund goal and monthly savings goal.
- Update the worksheet monthly with your contributions and adjust as needed to stay on track.

Step 5: Automate Your Savings

Automating your savings can help ensure consistent contributions to your emergency fund without having to remember to transfer funds each month.

Action Steps:

- Set up an automatic transfer from your checking account to your emergency fund savings account, scheduled around your payday.
- Adjust the transfer amount if your financial situation changes to either increase or maintain your savings rate.

Step 6: Review and Adjust Your Savings Plan

Regularly review your emergency fund and savings plan to adjust for any changes in your income, expenses, or financial goals.

Action Steps:

- Periodically reassess your living expenses and emergency fund goal to ensure it still meets your needs.
- If you receive a windfall or bonus, consider allocating a portion to your emergency fund to reach your goal sooner.

Conclusion

Building an emergency fund is a foundational aspect of personal finance that provides peace of mind and financial security. By determining your emergency fund goal, setting monthly savings targets, using a dedicated savings account, and tracking your progress with a savings goal worksheet, you can methodically build up your fund. Remember, the key is consistency and adaptability, adjusting your savings plan as your financial situation evolves to ensure that you're always prepared for the unexpected.

10.2 Planning for Long-Term Financial Health

Securing your financial future requires more than just saving money; it involves comprehensive planning and disciplined execution. This guide provides actionable steps for planning your long-term financial health, including a financial health checklist to help you systematically address the various components of a solid financial plan.

Step 1: Set Clear Financial Goals

The first step in planning for long-term financial health is to define your financial goals. These can range from short-term objectives like saving for a vacation to long-term goals like retirement or paying off a mortgage.

Action Steps:

- List your financial goals, categorizing them as short-term (1-3 years), medium-term (4-10 years), and long-term (10+ years).
- Be specific about what you want to achieve and by when, assigning a monetary value to each goal.

Step 2: Create a Detailed Budget

A detailed budget is essential for tracking income, expenses, and progress toward your financial goals.

Action Steps:

- Track your income and monthly expenses to understand where your money goes.
- Identify areas where you can cut back to allocate more towards your financial goals.
- Use budgeting software or a spreadsheet to monitor your budget regularly.

Step 3: Build an Emergency Fund

An emergency fund is crucial for long-term financial health, providing a safety net for unexpected expenses or income loss.

Action Steps:

- Aim to save at least 3-6 months' worth of living expenses.
- Open a separate savings account for your emergency fund and contribute to it regularly.

Step 4: Eliminate High-Interest Debt

High-interest debt, such as credit card debt, can hinder your financial progress. Prioritizing its repayment is key to improving your financial health.

Action Steps:

- List all your debts, noting the interest rate for each.
- Use the debt snowball or avalanche method to strategize repayments, focusing on high-interest debt first.

Step 5: Invest for the Future

Investing is essential for building wealth and achieving long-term financial goals like retirement.

Action Steps:

- Educate yourself on different investment options (stocks, bonds, mutual funds, real estate, etc.).
- Consider consulting a financial advisor to create an investment strategy that aligns with your risk tolerance and goals.
- Start contributing to retirement accounts, such as a 401(k) or IRA, taking advantage of employer matches if available.

Step 6: Protect Your Financial Future

Insurance and estate planning are critical for protecting your assets and ensuring your financial plan withstands unforeseen events.

Action Steps:

- Review your insurance needs (health, life, disability, property) to ensure adequate coverage.
- Start estate planning, including writing a will, designating beneficiaries, and considering a living trust.

Step 7: Use the Financial Health Checklist

A financial health checklist helps you systematically review and address key aspects of your financial plan.

Financial Health Checklist Components:

- **Financial Goals**: Review and update your financial goals regularly.
- **Budget and Spending**: Monitor your budget and adjust as needed.
- **Emergency Fund**: Track the growth of your emergency fund.
- **Debt Repayment**: Note progress in debt elimination.
- **Investments and Savings**: Regularly contribute to and review your investment accounts.
- **Insurance Coverage**: Ensure your insurance policies meet your current needs.
- **Estate Planning**: Keep your estate planning documents up to date.

Action Steps:

- Regularly complete the checklist to assess your financial health and identify areas needing attention.

Conclusion

Planning for long-term financial health is an ongoing process that requires attention to detail, discipline, and adaptability. By setting clear financial goals, creating a budget, building an emergency fund, eliminating debt, investing for the future, and protecting your financial future, you can establish a strong foundation for financial well-being. Regular use of the financial health checklist will help you stay on track and make informed decisions as your financial situation and goals evolve.

10.3 Continuous Learning and Adaptation

In an ever-evolving world, continuous learning and adaptation are key to personal and professional growth. This guide provides a structured approach to lifelong learning, emphasizing the importance of staying updated with new skills and knowledge. It includes a curated resource list for learning opportunities and a template for a personal development plan to help you track your progress.

Step 1: Assess Your Learning Goals

Start by identifying the areas in which you want to grow. These could be skills you wish to acquire for your current job, knowledge to help you pivot to a new career, or personal interests you want to explore.

Action Steps:

- Reflect on your career aspirations, hobbies, and interests to identify learning goals.
- Prioritize these goals based on their relevance to your long-term objectives and personal fulfillment.

Step 2: Identify Learning Resources

Once you have clear learning goals, the next step is to find resources that can help you achieve them. This can include online courses, books, podcasts, webinars, or in-person workshops.

Resource List Components:

- **Online Courses**: Websites like Coursera, edX, Udemy, and LinkedIn Learning offer courses on a wide range of subjects.
- **Books**: Identify key books that are well-regarded in your areas of interest.
- **Podcasts/Webinars**: Search for podcasts or webinars that cover relevant topics or industries.
- **Professional Networks**: Joining industry-specific networks or forums can provide insights and opportunities for mentorship.
- **Workshops/Seminars**: Look for local or virtual workshops and seminars that offer hands-on learning experiences.

Action Steps:

- Compile a list of resources that align with your learning goals.
- Schedule time in your week to engage with these resources.

Step 3: Create a Personal Development Plan

A personal development plan (PDP) helps you organize your learning objectives, action items, and timelines, making it easier to track your progress.

Personal Development Plan Components:

- **Learning Goal**: The skill or knowledge area you aim to develop.
- **Resources**: Specific resources you plan to use for this goal.
- **Action Steps**: Concrete steps you'll take to achieve your goal (e.g., complete a specific course, read a book, attend a workshop).
- **Timeline**: Set deadlines for completing each action step.
- **Progress Review**: Regular intervals to review your progress and adjust your plan as necessary.

Action Steps:

- Fill out the PDP template for each of your learning goals.
- Commit to regular reviews of your plan to assess your progress and make adjustments.

Step 4: Implement Your Learning Plan

With your PDP in place, start working towards your learning goals. Remember, the key to successful learning is consistency and application.

Action Steps:

- Begin engaging with the selected resources and following the action steps outlined in your PDP.
- Apply new knowledge or skills in practical settings whenever possible, whether in your current job, a personal project, or in volunteer opportunities.

Step 5: Reflect and Adapt

Continuous learning is an iterative process. Regular reflection on what you've learned and how it applies to your goals is essential for adapting your plan to fit your evolving needs.

Action Steps:

- Set aside time for regular reflections on what you've learned and how it applies to your personal and professional life.
- Update your PDP based on these reflections, adding new goals or resources as needed.

Conclusion

Continuous learning and adaptation are crucial for navigating the challenges and opportunities of the modern world. By assessing your learning goals, identifying relevant resources, creating a personal development plan, and committing to regular review and adaptation, you can ensure ongoing personal and professional growth. This structured approach not only enhances your skill set but also enriches your life, opening up new possibilities and pathways.

Conclusion

Recap of Key Savings Strategies: Your Roadmap to Financial Freedom

Achieving financial freedom is a goal for many, and it starts with effective savings strategies. This comprehensive guide offers a recap of essential savings tips and techniques, providing a clear roadmap to help you navigate your financial journey. Each section outlines actionable steps to implement these strategies, aiming to improve your financial health and move you closer to financial independence.

Assess and Understand Your Financial Situation

Action Steps:

1. **Track Your Spending**: Keep a detailed record of your income and expenses. Use budgeting apps or spreadsheets to categorize and analyze your spending habits.
2. **Set Financial Goals**: Define short-term and long-term financial goals, such as building an emergency fund, paying off debt, or saving for retirement.
3. **Create a Budget**: Based on your spending analysis and financial goals, develop a budget that allocates funds to essential expenses, savings, and debt repayment.

Reduce Expenses and Increase Savings

Action Steps:

1. **Cut Unnecessary Expenses**: Identify and eliminate non-essential spending. Focus on reducing discretionary expenses like dining out, subscriptions, and luxury items.
2. **Utilize Savings Tools**: Take advantage of coupons, discounts, and cashback apps to save on everyday purchases.

3. **Optimize Utility Costs**: Implement energy-saving measures to lower utility bills. Consider investing in energy-efficient appliances and home improvements.

Maximize Your Income

Action Steps:

1. **Seek Additional Income Streams**: Explore opportunities for side hustles, freelance work, or selling unused items.
2. **Invest in Your Career**: Pursue professional development to enhance your skills, seek promotions, or consider higher-paying job opportunities.
3. **Invest Wisely**: Educate yourself on investment options and consider starting with low-risk investments. Regularly contribute to retirement accounts to benefit from compound interest.

Manage Debt Efficiently

Action Steps:

1. **Prioritize High-Interest Debt**: Focus on paying off high-interest debts first, such as credit card balances, to reduce the total interest paid over time.
2. **Consolidate Debts**: If applicable, consider consolidating multiple debts into a single loan with a lower interest rate to simplify payments and potentially save on interest.
3. **Avoid New Debt**: Practice responsible spending and avoid taking on new debt unless absolutely necessary.

Plan for the Future

Action Steps:

1. **Build an Emergency Fund**: Aim to save at least 3-6 months' worth of living expenses to cover unexpected financial emergencies.

2. **Invest in Retirement**: Take advantage of employer-sponsored retirement plans or open an individual retirement account (IRA) to secure your financial future.
3. **Consider Insurance**: Ensure you have adequate insurance coverage (health, life, property) to protect against potential financial setbacks.

Continuously Learn and Adapt

Action Steps:

1. **Stay Informed**: Regularly educate yourself on financial matters, market trends, and new savings strategies.
2. **Review and Adjust Your Financial Plan**: Periodically reassess your financial goals, budget, and investment strategies to adapt to changes in your life or financial situation.
3. **Seek Professional Advice**: Consider consulting a financial advisor for personalized advice, especially for complex financial decisions.

Conclusion

Achieving financial freedom requires a combination of disciplined savings, wise spending, strategic income enhancement, efficient debt management, and future planning. By following this roadmap and continuously adapting your strategies to your evolving financial situation, you can build a solid foundation for financial independence and security. Remember, the journey to financial freedom is a marathon, not a sprint, requiring commitment, patience, and ongoing education.

Staying Motivated and Disciplined: A Checklist for Success

Achieving financial freedom requires not just a plan, but also the motivation and discipline to stick to that plan over time. Staying focused on your financial goals can be challenging, especially when faced with short-term temptations or setbacks. However, with the right mindset and strategies, you can maintain your motivation and discipline, ensuring long-term success. This guide provides a checklist to help you stay on track.

Set Clear, Achievable Goals

1. **Define Your Financial Goals**: Be specific about what you want to achieve, whether it's paying off debt, saving for a house, or building an emergency fund.
2. **Break Down Big Goals**: Divide larger goals into smaller, manageable milestones.
3. **Set Deadlines**: Having a timeline increases your sense of urgency and helps you stay focused.

Track Your Progress

1. **Keep a Financial Journal**: Regularly update your financial journal with progress towards your goals.
2. **Celebrate Milestones**: Recognize and celebrate when you reach a milestone, no matter how small.
3. **Adjust Goals as Necessary**: Be flexible and willing to adjust your goals based on changes in your financial situation or priorities.

Stay Educated

1. **Read Financial Literature**: Stay informed about financial strategies and trends by reading books, blogs, and articles.
2. **Attend Workshops and Seminars**: Engage in learning opportunities to enhance your financial knowledge.
3. **Use Financial Planning Tools**: Leverage apps and software to help you manage your finances more effectively.

Build a Support System

1. **Find a Financial Accountability Partner**: Share your goals with a trusted friend or family member who can help keep you accountable.
2. **Join Financial Support Groups**: Connect with others who are on similar financial journeys for mutual support and advice.
3. **Consult with Financial Professionals**: Seek advice from financial advisors or counselors when making significant financial decisions.

Practice Self-Care

1. **Manage Stress**: Engage in activities that reduce stress, as financial pressures can sometimes be overwhelming.
2. **Maintain a Healthy Lifestyle**: Good physical health supports mental clarity and decision-making.
3. **Remind Yourself of Your 'Why'**: Regularly remind yourself why achieving financial freedom is important to you.

Stay Disciplined

1. **Automate Savings and Payments**: Automating financial transactions can help maintain discipline without relying on willpower.
2. **Avoid Impulse Purchases**: Wait 24-48 hours before making significant purchases to ensure they align with your goals.
3. **Limit Exposure to Temptations**: Unsubscribe from marketing emails and avoid environments that encourage unnecessary spending.

Review and Reflect

1. **Conduct Monthly Financial Reviews**: Evaluate your spending, saving, and progress towards goals each month.
2. **Learn From Setbacks**: Instead of getting discouraged by setbacks, analyze them to understand what went wrong and how to avoid similar issues in the future.
3. **Adjust Your Plan as Needed**: Be willing to change your strategy if something isn't working or if your financial situation changes.

Checklist for Success:

- ✓ Clear financial goals with deadlines
- ✓ Regular progress tracking and milestone celebrations
- ✓ Continuous financial education
- ✓ Supportive accountability partner or group
- ✓ Regular self-care practices
- ✓ Automated savings and bill payments
- ✓ Monthly financial reviews
- ✓ Learning from setbacks
- ✓ Plan adjustments based on reflections

Staying motivated and disciplined in your journey to financial freedom is about setting clear goals, regularly reviewing your progress, educating yourself, and building a supportive environment. By following this checklist and adapting as you go, you can maintain your focus and achieve your financial objectives.

Appendices

A: Glossary of Personal Finance Terms

A

Annual Percentage Rate (APR): The annual rate charged for borrowing or earned through an investment, including any fees or additional costs associated with the transaction.

Assets: Anything of value owned by an individual, including cash, investments, property, and personal belongings.

B

Budget: A plan that outlines an individual's or household's expected income and expenses over a specific period, aiming to manage money effectively.

Bankruptcy: A legal process through which individuals or businesses unable to meet their debt obligations can seek relief from some or all of their debts.

C

Compound Interest: Interest calculated on the initial principal, which also includes all of the accumulated interest from previous periods on a deposit or loan.

Credit Score: A numerical expression based on a level analysis of a person's credit files, representing the creditworthiness of an individual.

D

Debt: Money owed by one party to another.

Deductible: The amount paid out of pocket by the policyholder before an insurance provider will pay any expenses.

E

Emergency Fund: Savings account designated for unexpected expenses or financial emergencies.

Equity: The value of an asset after deducting the amount of all liabilities on that asset.

F

Fixed Expenses: Costs that do not fluctuate with changes in production level or sales volume, such as rent, utilities, or loan payments.

Financial Freedom: The status of having enough income to pay for living expenses for the rest of one's life without having to be employed or dependent on others.

G

Gross Income: The total personal income before any deductions are made.

H

Health Savings Account (HSA): A tax-advantaged medical savings account available to taxpayers in the United States who are enrolled in a high-deductible health plan (HDHP).

I

Interest: The cost of borrowing money, typically expressed as an annual percentage of the principal.

Investment: An asset or item acquired with the goal of generating income or appreciation.

L

Liabilities: What a person or company owes to others—debts or obligations.

Liquidity: The ease with which an asset or security can be converted into ready cash without affecting its market price.

M

Mortgage: A loan taken out to buy property or land. The borrower agrees to make a predetermined set of payments to the lender.

Mutual Fund: An investment program funded by shareholders that trades in diversified holdings and is professionally managed.

N

Net Worth: The total assets minus total outside liabilities of an individual or a company.

P

Portfolio: A range of investments held by a person or organization.

Principal: The original sum of money borrowed in a loan, or put into an investment.

R

Retirement Plan: A financial arrangement designed to replace employment income upon retirement.

Risk Tolerance: An individual's capacity to endure loss in their investment values.

S

Savings Account: A bank account that earns interest.

Securities: Financial instruments that represent some type of financial value, such as stocks and bonds.

T

Tax Deduction: A reduction of income that is able to be taxed, thereby reducing the tax owed.

Term Life Insurance: Life insurance that provides coverage at a fixed rate of payments for a limited period.

U

Underwater Mortgage: A mortgage loan that has a higher principal than the free-market value of the home.

V

Variable Expenses: Costs that vary in proportion to the activity of a business or individual.

This glossary offers a foundation for understanding personal finance. However, the field of personal finance is broad and ever-evolving, and it may be beneficial to consult a financial advisor for advice tailored to your personal circumstances.

B. Creating a Budget

Creating and adhering to a budget is a foundational aspect of managing your finances effectively. A well-structured budget helps you track income, control expenditures, save for future goals, and ensure financial stability. This guide will provide you with a step-by-step approach to creating a budget using sample budgets and templates, making the process accessible and straightforward.

Step 1: Choose the Right Budgeting Method

The first step in budgeting is to select a method that suits your financial situation and goals. Popular methods include the 50/30/20 rule (needs/wants/savings), envelope system, zero-based budget, and the pay-yourself-first strategy.

Action Steps:

- Research each budgeting method to understand its principles and suitability for your circumstances.
- Decide on a method that aligns with your financial objectives and lifestyle.

Step 2: Assess Your Income and Expenses

Gather detailed information about your monthly income and expenses. This includes all sources of income after taxes and all fixed and variable expenses.

Action Steps:

- List all sources of monthly income, including salaries, bonuses, and any passive income.
- Compile a comprehensive list of monthly expenses, categorizing them into fixed (rent, utilities, insurance) and variable (groceries, entertainment, personal spending) expenses.

Step 3: Utilize a Budget Template

A budget template provides a structured format for organizing your income and expenses, making it easier to see where your money is going and where you can make adjustments.

Sample Budget Template Components:

- **Income Section**: List each source of income and the total monthly income.
- **Fixed Expenses Section**: Detail all fixed expenses with subtotals for housing, transportation, insurance, and other regular payments.
- **Variable Expenses Section**: List variable expenses, including food, entertainment, and personal spending, with a total for variable expenses.
- **Savings Goals Section**: Specify savings goals, such as emergency funds, retirement accounts, and other savings, with targeted amounts.
- **Summary**: A section to calculate the difference between total income and total expenditures, including savings.

Action Steps:

- Choose a budget template that complements your selected budgeting method or customize one to fit your needs.
- Fill in the template with your income and expenses data.

Step 4: Analyze and Adjust Your Budget

With your budget laid out in the template, analyze where your money is going and identify areas where adjustments can be made to align with your financial goals.

Action Steps:

- Review each category of expenses to identify non-essential spending that can be reduced or eliminated.
- Adjust your budget to increase savings and investments, aiming to meet or exceed your savings goals.

Step 5: Implement and Monitor Your Budget

Implement your budget by making the necessary adjustments to your spending habits. Regular monitoring is crucial to ensure adherence and to adjust for any changes in income or expenses.

Action Steps:

- Set up reminders to review your budget regularly (e.g., weekly or monthly).
- Track your actual spending against the budgeted amounts and adjust as needed.

Step 6: Review and Revise Periodically

Your financial situation and goals will evolve over time, necessitating periodic reviews and revisions of your budget.

Action Steps:

- Schedule quarterly or bi-annual reviews of your budget to reflect any significant changes in income, expenses, or financial goals.
- Update your budget template to accommodate these changes and set new financial priorities as necessary.

Conclusion

Budgeting is an ongoing process that requires commitment, discipline, and regular review. By choosing a suitable budgeting method, utilizing a comprehensive budget template, and consistently monitoring your financial progress, you can achieve greater control over your finances, meet your savings goals, and work towards long-term financial stability and success.

C. Quick Reference: Summary of Action Steps and Worksheets

Creating a sound financial plan involves a series of strategic actions and the use of various tools and worksheets to organize and track your progress. This guide offers a concise summary of essential action steps across different financial planning areas, along with references to key worksheets that will assist you in achieving your financial goals.

Setting Financial Goals

Action Steps:

1. **Identify Short-term and Long-term Goals**: Distinguish between immediate financial priorities and long-term aspirations.
2. **Quantify Goals**: Assign specific monetary values to each goal for clarity.
3. **Set Deadlines**: Establish realistic timeframes for achieving each goal.

Worksheet: Goals Worksheet

- List each goal with its value and deadline for a clear roadmap of your financial aspirations.

Budgeting and Expense Tracking

Action Steps:

1. **Assess Monthly Income**: Calculate your total monthly income from all sources.
2. **Categorize Expenses**: Divide your expenses into fixed and variable categories.
3. **Adjust Spending**: Identify areas for cost-saving and adjust your budget accordingly.

Worksheet: Monthly Budget Template

- Organize your income and expenses into categories for easy tracking and adjustment.

Saving and Investing

Action Steps:

1. **Determine Saving Objectives**: Define specific saving goals, such as an emergency fund, retirement, or large purchases.
2. **Choose Investment Vehicles**: Research and select appropriate investment options based on risk tolerance and time horizon.
3. **Regularly Contribute**: Set up automatic transfers to savings and investment accounts.

Worksheet: Savings and Investment Tracker

- Track contributions and growth in savings and investment accounts, aligned with your financial objectives.

Debt Management

Action Steps:

1. **List All Debts**: Compile details of all debts, including amounts, interest rates, and due dates.
2. **Prioritize Repayment**: Focus on high-interest debts or use the snowball method for motivation.
3. **Negotiate Terms**: Contact lenders to discuss potential for better terms or consolidation options.

Worksheet: Debt Repayment Plan

- Outline a strategy for debt repayment, including prioritized debts and monthly payment amounts.

Emergency Fund

Action Steps:

1. **Calculate Desired Fund Size**: Aim for 3-6 months of living expenses.
2. **Start Small**: Begin saving a manageable amount regularly.
3. **Review and Adjust**: Increase contributions as your financial situation improves.

Worksheet: Emergency Fund Tracker

- Monitor the growth of your emergency fund against your target amount.

Credit Score Improvement

Action Steps:

1. **Check Credit Reports**: Obtain and review your credit reports for inaccuracies.
2. **Pay Bills on Time**: Ensure timely payment of all bills.
3. **Reduce Credit Utilization**: Pay down outstanding balances and avoid maxing out credit lines.

Worksheet: Credit Improvement Log

- Keep a record of actions taken to improve your credit score, including disputes filed and debts paid off.

Insurance and Estate Planning

Action Steps:

1. **Review Insurance Needs**: Assess necessary coverage for health, life, and property.
2. **Update Estate Documents**: Ensure wills, trusts, and beneficiary designations are current.
3. **Consider Future Expenses**: Plan for long-term care and other later-life expenses.

Worksheet: Insurance Coverage and Estate Planning Checklist

- Document your insurance policies and estate planning steps, including policy details and key contacts.

Conclusion

Achieving financial stability and growth requires ongoing effort across various aspects of personal finance. By following these summarized action steps and utilizing the corresponding worksheets, you can create a structured approach to managing your finances, tracking your progress, and adjusting your strategies as needed to meet your changing financial landscape.